Dear Virginia,
Just to get
you back into
the rhythm of
Australian life.

Love Kim Peter
Jamie & Kelly

Sept '87.

GW00566299

THE ALL-TIME FAVOURITE AUSTRALIAN SONG BOOK

THE ALL-TIME FAVOURITE AUSTRALIAN SONG BOOK

Illustrated by
PATRICK COOK

ANGUS & ROBERTSON PUBLISHERS

Unit 4, Eden Park, 31 Waterloo Road,
North Ryde, NSW, Australia 2113
and
16 Golden Square, London W1R 4BN, United Kingdom

First published in Australia by Angus & Robertson Publishers in 1984
First published in the United Kingdom by Angus & Robertson (UK) Ltd in 1984

Copyright © This collection and presentation Angus & Robertson Publishers 1984

National Library of Australia
Cataloguing-in-publication data.
The All-time favourite Australian song book.
  Includes index.
  ISBN 0 207 14755 8.
  1. Songs, English — Australia — Texts. I. Cook, Patrick, 1949-
784'.0994

Typeset in 10pt Goudy Old Style Roman by Setrite Typesetters
Printed in Hong Kong by Everbest Printing Co., Ltd

Publisher's Note

The convicts originally brought with them to Sydney Cove a love of traditional English and Irish ballads and sea shanties, and no doubt this simple music provided one of their few solaces on that otherwise desolate shore. In time, of course, they added to their repertoire songs of their own invention, some sentimental and yearning, others giving voice to the self-mockery that has become so characteristically Australian.

It was Banjo Paterson who first systematically collected nineteenth-century indigenous bush songs, and then, seventy years later, groups like the Bushwhackers Band popularised them all over again so successfully that it is almost too easy to fall into the trap of believing that the Australian popular ballad died with Lawson and Paterson.

As this collection makes evident, over a period of time the ballad's province in fact widened. Ultimately, it could sing the praises of both Tenterfield saddlers and Newcastle rockers; it could be maudlin, or raucous, or satirical; it could be composed by country musicians or city jinglesmiths.

It becomes clear that the modern songs are somewhat less earnest than their predecessors. Although no-one today would dare compose anything remotely like "God Bless Australia", the nationalistic mood is nonetheless pervasive and fervent. The rhythms and rhymes are rough, and the style is often declamatory.

We have brought together here in one volume all the songs, ancient and modern, that today's Australians like to sing about themselves. Mostly the tunes are sufficiently familiar that no-one needs to have the music provided, and the space, not to mention cost, that reproducing such music might have required could thus be given over completely to Patrick Cook's extraordinary and whimsical illuminations.

The result — depending on your point of view — is an entertaining and witty collection of musical verse, a timely piece of folk research, an essential family reference book, or an aide-mémoire for the next communal singalong.

Acknowledgements

For kind permission to use the songs included in this collection Angus & Robertson Publishers acknowledge with thanks the following:

J. Albert & Son Pty Ltd for "I'm Going Back to Yarrawonga".

Allans Music Australia Pty Ltd for "Advance Australia Fair", "Along the Road to Gundagai", "Bourke Street on Saturday Night", "God Bless Australia", "Goodbye, Melbourne Town", "Hustling Hinkler", "My Old Black Billy", "Our Don Bradman", "The Snake Gully Swagger", "The Song of Australia", "Waltzing Matilda" and "Where the Dog Sits on the Tucker Box".

Pat Alexander for "Duncan".

ATV Northern Songs Pty Ltd for "Is 'E an Aussie?".

April Music Pty Ltd for "Down Under".

Avenue Records for "Wangaratta Wahine".

Belinda Music Australia Pty Ltd (and Castle Music Pty Ltd) for "I've Been Everywhere".

Bill Cate for "Santa Never Made It into Darwin".

Castle Music Pty Ltd for "Tie Me Kangaroo Down, Sport", "Six White Boomers", "Stompin' at Maroubra".

Castlemaine Tooheys Ltd (and Mojo Australia) for "I Feel Like a Tooheys".

Chappell & Co. (Australia) Pty Ltd for "Carol of the Birds", "Christmas Day", "The Silver Stars Are in the Sky", "The Three Drovers", "Christmas Bush for His Adorning".

John Clarke for "We Don't Know How Lucky We Are".

Essex Music of Australia Pty Ltd for "The 'Goondiwindi Grey'".

Fairydust Music for "Silver City Birthday Celebration Day".

General Motors-Holden and George Patterson Pty Ltd for "We Love Football, Meat Pies, Kangaroos and Holden Cars".

Bob Hudson and Chris Neal for "Rack Off Normie".

Barry Humphries for "The Old Pacific Sea", "Edna's Hymn" and "Edna's Favourite Things".

Ida Elizabeth Jenkins for "The Argonauts' Club Song" and ABC Children's Session Opening Song and Goodnight Song.

Intersong Pty Ltd (and Chappell & Co. [Australia] Pty Ltd) for "Tenterfield Saddler".

Eric Jupp for "My Pal Skippy".

Kraft Foods Limited for "We're Happy Little Vegemites".

Larrikin Records for "Australia Square", "Rose Bay Ferry", and "The Band Played Waltzing Matilda".

Leeds Music Pty Ltd for "Little Boy Lost", "My Boomerang Won't Come Back", "The Newcastle Song" and (with Cincom Music) "My City of Sydney".

Matthews Music for "Here Come the Aussies".

Nicholson's Pty Ltd for "A Pub with No Beer".

Razzle Music (with Festival Music Pty Ltd) for "Howzat".

Remix Music Pty Ltd for "Up There Cazaly" and "Shaddap You Face".

Rondor Music (Australia) Pty Ltd for "I Still Call Australia Home".

Summertime Music for "Have You Ever Been to See Kings Cross?".

Traders Pty Ltd for "The Aeroplane Jelly Song".

Warner Bros Music Australia Pty Ltd for "Come On, Aussie, Come On".

Yeldah Music for "Red-back on the Toilet Seat".

Our warmest thanks also to all writers and/or publishers who contributed so cheerfully and generously the introductions and notes to the songs they helped make all-time Australian favourites.

"Up jumped the swagman..."

Contents

HEAVE AWAY,
HAUL AWAY

Botany Bay

Folklorist John S. Manifold in his Australian Song Book has described "Botany Bay" as "the nadir of flippant vulgarity" and "a parody of genuine convict songs". The song was to top the pops in this country in 1886 when comedian David Belasco Jones introduced wider audiences to it as part of a musical comedy called Little Jack Shepherd.

Farewell to old England forever,
Farewell to my rum culls as well;
Farewell to the well-known Old Bailey,
Where I used for to cut such a swell.

Chorus:
Singing too-ral li-ooral li-ad-dity
Singing too-ral li-ooral li-ay;
Singing too-ral li-ooral li-ad-dity
Singing too-ral li-ooral li-ay.

There's the Captain as is our Commander,
There's the bo'sun and all the ship's crew,
There's the first and the second-class passengers,
Knows what we poor convicts go through.

'Tain't leavin' old England we cares about,
'Tain't cos we miss pals what we knows,
But becos all we light-fingered gentry
Hops around with a log on our toes.

For seven long years I'll be staying here,
For seven long years and a day,
For meeting a cove in an area
And taking his ticker away.

Oh, had I the wings of a turtle-dove!
I'd soar on my pinions so high,
Slap bang to the arms of my Polly love,
And in her sweet presence I'd die.

Now, all my young Dookies and Duchesses,
Take warning from what I've to say,
Mind all is your own as you touchesses,
Or you'll find us in Botany Bay.

Anon.

Bound for South Australia

*Sung originally as a sea shanty, there were two slightly different versions of this song.
One was chanted in slow rhythm to the heavy work of winding the capstan. The other
was relatively quicker and timed for halyard work, the hoisting and lowering of sails.*

Solo: In South Australia I was born —
Chorus: Heave away! haul away!
Solo: South Australia round Cape Horn,
Chorus: Bound for South Australia.

Chorus:
Heave away you ruler kings —
Heave away, haul away,
Heave away, you'll hear me sing,
Bound for South Australia.

There's one thing there that grieves my mind —
It's leaving Nancy Blair behind.

I'll tell you the truth and tell you no lie —
I'll love that girl till the day I die.

As I was walloping around Cape Horn —
I'd wished to God, I'd never been born.

And now I'm on a foreign strand —
With a bottle of whisky in my hand.

I'll drink one glass to the foreign shore —
And another to the girl that I adore.

Fare thee well, and fare thee well —
And sweet news to my girl I'll tell.

Anon.

Moreton Bay

Some attribute authorship of this haunting ballad to Frank the Poet alias Frank McNamara alias Francis Goddard, a convict transported in the 1820s. The tune is an old Irish air and it is probable that the song had wide currency among dissatisfied Irish settlers. Ned Kelly uses lines very similar to it in his Jerilderie Letter. Captain Logan did exist and doubtless there were few at Moreton Bay who mourned when in October 1830 news of his being speared to death was heard.

One Sunday morning as I was walking,
By Brisbane waters I chanced to stray,
I heard a convict his fate bewailing
As on the sunny river bank he lay:
"I am a native of Erin's island
Transported now from my native shore,
They tore me from my aged parents
And from the maiden that I do adore.

"I've been a convict at Port Macquarie,
At Norfolk Island and Emu Plains,
At Castle Hill and cursed Toongabbie,
At all those settlements I've worked in chains;
But of all places of condemnation
And penal stations of New South Wales,
To Moreton Bay I have found no equal;
Excessive tyranny each day prevails.

"For three long years I was beastly treated
And heavy irons on my leg I wore;
My back with floggings was lacerated,
And often painted with my crimson gore.
And many a man from downright starvation
Lies mouldering now beneath the clay;
And Captain Logan he had us mangled
At the triangles of Moreton Bay.

"Like the Egyptians and ancient Hebrews
We were oppressed under Logan's yoke,
Till a native black lying there in ambush
Did deal our tyrant his mortal stroke.
My fellow prisoners, be exhilarated
That all such monsters such a death may find,
And when from bondage we are liberated,
Our former sufferings shall fade from mind."

Frank the Poet

The Girl with the Black Velvet Band

There are several slightly different versions of this song which appears to have been first aired in about 1842.

'Twas in the city of London,
In 'prenticeship I was bound
And many's the gay old hour
I spent in that dear old town.
One day as I was walking
Along my usual beat
A pretty little young maiden
Came tripping along the street.

Chorus:
And her eyes they shone like diamonds,
I thought her the pride of the land;
The hair that hung down to her shoulder
Was tied with a black velvet band.

One day as we were a-walking
A gentleman passed us by;
I could see she was bent on some mischief
By the rolling of her dark blue eye.
Gold watch she picked from his pocket
And slyly placed into my hand;
I was taken in charge by a copper,
Bad luck to that black velvet band.

Before the Lord Mayor I was taken,
"Your case, sir, I plainly can see,
And, if I'm not greatly mistaken
You're bound far over the sea."
It's over the dark and blue ocean,
Far away to Van Diemen's Land,
Away from my friends and relations
And the girl with the black velvet band.

Anon.

The Wild Colonial Boy

The origins of this song are obscure, though versions are sung in Ireland, America and Britain. There is no historical trace of an outlaw corresponding in name or deed. There was, however, a Judge Macoboy and, while Macoboy family legend confirms the robbery, as far as it's known, his honour was not accosted by "gentlemen of the road".

There was a Wild Colonial Boy,
Jack Doolan was his name,
Of poor but honest parents
He was born in Castlemaine.
He was his father's only hope,
His mother's pride and joy
And dearly did his parents love
The Wild Colonial Boy.

Chorus:
So come away me hearties
We'll roam the mountains high,
Together we will plunder
And together we will die.
We'll scour along the valleys
And we'll gallop o'er the plains,
And scorn to live in slavery,
Bound down by iron chains.

At the age of sixteen years
He left his native home
And to Australia's sunny shores,
A bushranger did roam.
They put him in the iron gang
In the government employ,
But never an iron on earth could hold
The Wild Colonial Boy.

In '61 this daring youth
Commenced his wild career,
With a heart that knew no danger
And no foeman did he fear.
He stuck up the Beechworth mail coach
And robbed Judge Macoboy
Who, trembling cold, gave up his gold
To the Wild Colonial Boy.

He bade the Judge good morning
And he told him to beware,
That he'd never rob a needy man
Or one who acted square,
But a Judge who'd rob a mother
Of her one and only joy
Sure, he must be a worse outlaw than
The Wild Colonial Boy.

One day as Jack was riding
The mountainside along,
A-listening to the little birds,
Their happy laughing song.
Three mounted troopers came along,
Kelly, Davis and Fitzroy
With a warrant for the capture of
The Wild Colonial Boy.

"Surrender now! Jack Doolan,
For you see it's three to one;
Surrender in the Queen's own name.
You are a highwayman."
Jack drew a pistol from his belt
And waved it like a toy,
"I'll fight, but not surrender," cried
The Wild Colonial Boy.

He fired at trooper Kelly
And brought him to the ground,
And in return from Davis
Received a mortal wound,
All shattered through the jaws he lay
Still firing at Fitzroy.
And that's the way they captured him,
The Wild Colonial Boy.

Anon.

ON THE TRACK

Rover No More

*One of the most popular folksongs in the English language, with versions to be found in
every English-speaking country. The first Australian version was collected by ''Banjo''
Paterson in 1905 and published in his* Old Bush Songs.

I've been a wild rover this many a year;
I spent all my money on whisky and beer.
But now I'll give over, my money I'll store,
And I'll play the wild rover, wild rover no more.

Chorus:
Nay, no, never! never no more!
I shall play the wild rover, wild rover no more.

I went to a shanty I used to frequent,
And I told the landlady my money was spent.
I asked her for credit, she answered me "Nay,
Such custom as yours I can get any day."

Then out of my pocket I drew sovereigns bright;
The landlady opened her eyes at the sight!
She said "I have whisky and wines of the best,
For the things I was saying were only in jest."

I'll go to my parents, tell them what I've done,
And beg them to pardon their prodigal son;
And if they forgive me as they've done before,
I shall play the wild rover, wild rover no more.

Anon.

With My Swag All On My Shoulder

The discovery of gold attracted many free settlers to Australia in the 1850s. Many of those who were unsuccessful prospectors ended up shouldering a swag and taking to the road, moving from one property to the next in search of food, work and shelter.

When first I left old Ireland's shore,
The yarns that I was told,
Of how folks in Australia
Could dig up lumps of gold,
How gold dust lay in all the streets
And the miner's right was free.
Hurrah, says I, my loving friends
That's just the place for me.

Chorus:
With my swag all on my shoulder,
Black billy in my hand,
I'll travel the bush of Australia,
Like a true-born native man.

And then we came to Melbourne town,
We all prepared to slip,
All bar the captain and the mate
All the crew abandoned ship,
And all the girls of Melbourne town
Threw up their hands with joy,
Sayin' one unto the other,
Here comes my Irish boy.

We made our way to Geelong town,
And north-west to Ballarat,
Where some of us grew mighty thin,
And some grew sleek and fat.
Some tried their luck at Bendigo
And some at Fiery Creek —
I made my fortune in a day,
And blued it in a week.

For many a long year I have travelled round
To each new field about.
I have made and spent full many a pound,
Till the alluvial petered out,
And now for any job of work
I am prepared to try
But now I've found the tucker track
I'll stay here till I die.

Anon.

11

My Old Black Billy

Written by poet Edward Harrington and set to the music of Roy Jeffries in 1940, "My Old Black Billy" was to find enduring popularity when in 1953 it was included in the musical Reedy River. This play with a trade union base about a group of shearers in the old days included many old bush songs of the 1800s and is without doubt Australia's most popular musical. It is still performed and now as when first performed the haunting stillness of "My Old Black Billy" is an emotion-filled show stopper.

I have humped my bluey in all the states,
With my old black billy, the best of mates,
For years I have camped and toiled and tramped,
On the roads that are rough and hilly,
With my plain and sensible, indispensable
Old black billy.

Chorus:
My old black billy, my old black billy,
Whether the wind is warm or chilly,
I always find when the shadows fall
My old black billy's the best mate of all.

I have carried my swag on the parched Paroo,
Where water is scarce, and the houses few,
On many a track on the great outback,
Where the heat would drive you silly,
I have carried my sensible, indispensable
Old black billy.

When the days of tramping at last are o'er,
And I drop my swag at the Golden Door,
Saint Peter will stare when he sees me there,
Then he'll say "Poor Wand'ring Willie,
Come in with your sensible, indispensable
Old black billy."

Edward Harrington

The Overlander

There are different versions of both song and tune. The version given here is that first collected by John Manifold who learnt it at his father's knee. The tune is as you like it.

There's a trade you all know well,
It's bringing cattle over.
On every track, to the Gulf and back,
Men know the Queensland drover.

Chorus:
Pass the billy round, my boys!
Don't let the pint-pot stand there!
For tonight we drink the health
Of every overlander.

I come from the northern plains
Where the girls and grass are scanty;
Where the creeks run dry or ten foot high
And it's either drought or plenty.

There are men from every land,
From Spain and France and Flanders;
They're a well-mixed pack, both white and black,
The Queensland overlanders.

When we've earned a spree in town
We live like pigs in clover;
And the whole year's cheque pours down the neck
Of many a Queensland drover.

As I pass along the roads,
The children raise my dander
Crying "Mother dear, take in the clothes,
Here comes an overlander!"

Now I'm bound for home once more,
On a prad that's quite a goer;
I can find a job with a crawling mob
On the banks of the Maranoa.

Anon.

The Dying Stockman

There are songs on this theme throughout the English-speaking world — "The Streets of Laredo" being a popular example. In Australia, poet Adam Lindsay Gordon was first to use the image of death outback in verse in his "The Sick Stockrider".
Folklorist Bill Scott records receiving a letter which accredited authorship of this song to Horace Alfred Flower "who wrote these words in Gatton in 1892". This haunting version has endured despite a number of bawdy parodies more than somewhat unsuitable for inclusion in a family collection of this nature.

A strapping young stockman lay dying,
His saddle supporting his head;
His two mates around him were crying,
As he rose on his pillow and said:

Chorus:
"Wrap me up with my stockwhip and blanket,
And bury me deep down below,
Where dingoes and crows can't molest me,
In the shade where the coolibahs grow."

"Oh, had I the flight of the bronzewing,
Far o'er the plains would I fly,
Straight to the land of my childhood,
And there would I lay down and die."

"Then cut down a couple of saplings,
Place one at my head and my toe,
Carve on them cross, stockwhip and saddle,
To show there's a stockman below."

"Hark! there's the wail of a dingo,
Watchful and weird — I must go,
For it tolls the death-knell of the stockman,
From the gloom of the scrub down below."

"There's tea in the battered old billy;
Place the pannikins out in a row,
And we'll drink to the next merry meeting,
In the place where all good fellows go."

"And oft in the shades of the twilight,
When the soft winds are whispering low,
And the darkening shadows are falling,
Sometimes think of the stockman below."

Anon.

14

Waltzing Matilda

Written by Banjo Paterson in 1895 when on a visit to Dagworth Station near Winton in central western Queensland, "Waltzing Matilda" has become Australia's unofficial national song. In his biography The Banjo of the Bush, *Clement Semmler writes of it, "The words satisfy a certain instinct for nationalism: every Australian knows what 'waltzing Matilda', 'jumbuck', 'tucker-bag', and 'billabong' mean, so that the song is almost a password in foreign countries. And the elements of 'fair go', of the little man against the big man, of anti-authority, of bravado and of the setting of the outback give the song that added appeal to the average Australian conscious of his colonial beginnings."*

Once a jolly swagman camp'd by a billabong,
Under the shade of a coolibah tree,
And he sang as he watch'd and waited till his billy boiled
You'll come a waltzing Matilda with me.

Chorus:
Waltzing Matilda, Waltzing Matilda,
You'll come a waltzing Matilda with me,
And he sang as he watched and waited till his billy boiled
You'll come a waltzing Matilda with me.

Down came a jumbuck to drink at that billabong,
Up jumped the swagman and grabbed him with glee,
And he sang as he shoved that jumbuck in his tuckerbag
You'll come a waltzing Matilda with me.

Waltzing Matilda, Waltzing Matilda,
You'll come a waltzing Matilda with me,
And he sang as he shoved that jumbuck in his tuckerbag,
You'll come a waltzing Matilda with me.

Up rode the squatter mounted on his thoroughbred,
Down came the troopers, one, two, three,
Whose is that jolly jumbuck you've got in your tuckerbag?
You'll come a waltzing Matilda with me.

Waltzing Matilda, Waltzing Matilda,
You'll come a waltzing Matilda with me,
Whose is that jolly jumbuck you've got in your tuckerbag?
You'll come a waltzing Matilda with me.

Up jumped the swagman, sprang into the billabong,
You'll never catch me alive said he,
And his ghost may be heard as you pass by that billabong
You'll come a waltzing Matilda with me.

Waltzing Matilda, Waltzing Matilda,
You'll come a waltzing Matilda with me,
And his ghost may be heard as you pass by that billabong,
You'll come a waltzing Matilda with me.

Adapted from A. B. ("Banjo") Paterson

The Drover's Dream

This appears to be a reasonably recent addition to the folklorists' repertoire and several lay claim to its collection. Douglas Stewart and David Campbell recorded a session with a shearer and shearers' cook in Gundagai, New South Wales. John Callaghan and Bill Scott collected a version from "a fellow called Albert Stacey of Cloncurry who said he had learned it from a shearers' cook called 'The Pelican'". Shearers' cooks, it would seem, have temperaments a lot sweeter than that in the portrait left to us by Henry Lawson in "The Shearing of the Cook's Dog".

One night while droving sheep, my companions lay asleep,
There was not a star to 'luminate the sky,
I was dreaming I suppose, for my eyes were partly closed,
When a very strange procession passed me by.
First there came a kangaroo, with his swag of blankets blue,
A dingo ran beside him as a mate;
They were travelling mighty fast,
But they shouted as they passed:
"We'll have to jog along, it's getting late."

The pelican and the crane they came in from off the plain
To amuse the company with a Highland fling;
The dear old bandicoot played the tune upon his flute,
And the native bears sat round them in a ring.
The brolga and the crow sang us songs of long ago,
The frill-necked lizard listened with a smile,
And the emu standing near
With his claw up to his ear
Said, "That's the funniest thing I've heard for quite a while."

The frogs from out the swamp where the atmosphere is damp,
Came bounding in and sat upon some stones;
They all unrolled their swags and produced from little bags,
The violin, the banjo and the bones.
The goanna and the snake and the adder, wide awake,
With an alligator danced the "Soldier's Joy";
In the spreading silky oak
The jackass cracked a joke,
And the magpie sang "The Wild Colonial Boy".

Some wombats darted out from the ti-tree all about,
And performed a set of Lancers very well;
The parrot green and blue gave the orchestra its cue
To strike up the "Old Log Cabin in the Dell".
I was dreaming I suppose of these entertaining shows,
But it never crossed my mind I was asleep,
Till the boss beneath the cart
Woke me up with such a start
Yellin', "Dreamy, where the hell are all the sheep?"

Anon.

The Old Bullock Dray

Banjo Paterson was first to collect this ballad and his notes are illuminating. "Calling at the depot" to get an offsider meant picking out a wife from the new female immigrants who were housed at the depot on arrival. Such a wife, the minstrel planned, would be his assistant driver, the one who walks and flogs the bullocks when necessary.
Thus here we have Australia's version of "Come Live With Me and Be My Love".
Though indeed in Donne's poem the poet offers passion (possibly unlawful) and romance and our bullocky offers work security and marriage — the parallels are there to be drawn (and wept over).

Chorus:
So it's roll up your blankets,
And let's make a push,
I'll take you up the country,
And show you the bush.
I'll be bound you won't get
Such a chance another day,
So come and take possession
Of my old bullock dray.

Oh! the shearing is all over,
And the wool is coming down,
And I mean to get a wife, boys,
When I go up to town.
Everything that has two legs
Represents itself in view,
From the little paddymelon
To the bucking kangaroo.

Now, I've saved up a good cheque,
I mean to buy a team,
And when I get a wife, boys,
I'll be all-serene;
For, calling at the depot,
They say there's no delay
To get an offsider
For the old bullock dray.

Oh! we'll live like fighting cocks,
For good living, I'm your man.
We'll have leather-jacks, johnny-cakes,
And fritters in the pan;
Or if you'd like some fish
I'll catch you some soon,
For we'll bob for barramundies
Round the banks of a lagoon.

Oh! yes, of beef and damper
I take care we have enough,
And we'll boil in the bucket
Such a whopper of a duff,
And our friends will dance
To the honour of the day,
To the music of the bells
Around the old bullock dray.

Oh! we'll have plenty girls,
We must mind that.
There'll be flash little Maggie,
And buckjumping Pat.
There'll be Stringybark Joe,
And Greenhide Mike.
Yes, my colonials, just
As many as you like.

Now we'll stop all immigration,
We won't need it any more;
We'll be having young natives,
Twins by the score.
And I wonder what the devil
Jack Robertson would say
If he saw us promenading
Round the old bullock dray.

Oh! it's time I had an answer,
If there's one to be had,
I wouldn't treat that steer
In the body half as bad;
But he takes as much notice
Of me, upon my soul,
As that old blue stag
Offside in the pole.

Oh! to tell a lot of lies,
You know, it is a sin,
But I'll go up country
And marry a black gin.
Oh! "Baal gammon white feller",
This is what she'll say,
"Budgery you
And your old bullock dray."

Anon.

18

Along the Road to Gundagai

When first published in 1922 this song established the fame of Jack O'Hagan. By the end of that year, after 100,000 copies had been sold, it had doubtless contributed towards establishing his fortune as well. With its evocative scenes of bush shacks and waiting family and friends it became a popular World War II song, and was a happy choice of theme for the long-running radio show Dad and Dave *based on Steele Rudd's legendary yarns of selection life.*

There's a scene that lingers in my memory —
Of an old bush home and friends I long to see —
That's why I am yearning
Just to be returning
Along the road to Gundagai —

Chorus:
There's a track winding back
To an old-fashioned shack
Along the road to Gundagai —
Where the blue gums are growing
And the Murrumbidgee's flowing
Beneath that sunny sky —
Where my daddy and mother
Are waiting for me
And the pals of my childhood
Once more I will see.
Then no more will I roam,
When I'm heading right for home
Along the road to Gundagai.

When I get back there I'll be a kid again —
Oh! I'll never have a thought of grief or pain —
Once more I'll be playing
Where the gums are swaying
Along the road to Gundagai —

Jack O'Hagan

Tenterfield Saddler

In 1972, when this song was first published, Peter Allen had been living away from Australia for many years. He had made the big time in the Big Apple they call New York, he was writing and performing songs successfully and he had married Liza Minelli, "the girl with an interesting face". Far removed indeed from his roots in the dry north of New South Wales. But in this loving tribute to his forebears, he revealed he had not moved so far along the track that he could not return, in spirit at least, to the people and places of his youth.

The late George Woolnough worked High Street an' lived on manners.
Fifty-two years he sat on his veranda and made his saddles,
And if you had questions 'bout sheep or flowers or dogs,
You'd just ask the Saddler.
He lived without sin;
They're building a libr'y for him.

> *Chorus:*
> Time is a traveller,
> Tenterfield Saddler, turn your head.
> Ride again, jackaroo;
> Think I see kangaroo up ahead.

The son of George Woolnough went off and got married, and had a
  war baby,
Though something was wrong — and it's easier to drink than go crazy.
And if there were questions about why the end was so sad, well,
George had no answers about why a son ever has need of a gun.

The grandson of George has been all around the world and lives no
  special place,
Changed his last name and he married a girl with an int'resting face.
He'd almost forgotten them both, because in the life that he leads
There's nowhere for George and his libr'y or the son with his gun
To belong, except in this song.

> *(Vocal Ad Lib)*
>
> Time is a meddler
> Tenterfield Saddler,
> Make your bed.
> Fly away, cockatoo;
> Down on the ground, emu
> Up ahead.
>   Peter Allen

I've Been Everywhere

*Tasteless rock and roll was the beginning of this song. "I was in the car, irritably listening
to the radio," Geoff Mack recalls. "I remember thinking I should write a 12-bar with
practically no tune at all. At the same time I glanced at three road maps — Queensland,
New South Wales and Victoria... In two hours I had it written."*

I was humpin' my bluey along the dusty Oodnadatta road,
When along came a semi with a high and canvas-covered load.
"If you're goin' to Oodnadatta, mate, with me you can ride."
So I climbed in the cabin and then I settled down inside.
He asked me if I'd seen a road with so much dust and sand, and I said
"Listen, mate, I've travelled ev'ry road in this here land."

Chorus:
"I've been everywhere, man,
I've been everywhere, man.
'Cross the deserts bare, man.
I've breathed the mountain air, man.
Of travel I've had my share, man.
I've been everywhere.
I know some place you haven't been,
I've been everywhere."

Chant:
Been to —
Tullamore, Seymour, Lismore, Mooloolaba,
Nambour, Maroochydore, Kilmore, Murwillumbah.
Birdsville, Emmaville, Wallaville, Cunnamulla,
Condamine, Strathpine, Proserpine, Ulladulla,
Darwin, Gin Gin, Deniliquin, Muckadilla,
Wallambilla, Boggabilla, Kumbarilla, I'm a killer.

Moree, Taree, Jerilderie, Bambaroo,
Toowoomba, Gunnedah, Caringbah, Woolloomooloo.
Dalveen, Tamborine, Engadine, Jindabyne,
Lithgow, Casino, Brigalow, Narromine,
Megalong, Wyong, Tuggerawong, Wanganella,
Morella, Augathella, Brindabella, I'm the feller.

Wollongong, Geelong, Kurrajong, Mullumbimby,
Mittagong, Molong, Grong Grong, Goondiwindi,
Yarra Yarra, Bouindarra, Wallangarra, Turramurra,
Boggabri, Gundagai, Narrabri, Tibooburra,
Gulgong, Adelong, Billabong, Cabramatta,
Parramatta, Wangaratta, Coolangatta, what's it matter?

Ettalong, Dandenong, Woodenbong, Ballarat,
Canberra, Unanderra, Captain's Flat,
Cloncurry, River Murray, Kurri Kurri, Girraween,
Terrigal, Fingal, Stockinbingal, Collaroy and Narrabeen,
Bendigo, Dorrigo, Bangalow, Indooroopilly,
Kirribilli, Yeerongpilly, Wollondilly, don't be silly.

Geoff Mack

Rose Bay Ferry

Bernard Bolan recalls: "I used to live in Rose Bay a few years ago. Every morning we would get on board, we businessmen with our dark suits and our briefcases. There would always be one group of weekend sailors who discussed in loud voices the prevailing wind and what it was going to be like 'out in the middle' today. You would have thought we were taking a clipper across to San Diego.
To those brave men, battling the mountainous watery chasms between Rose Bay and Circular Quay, was the song dedicated."

Every morning at eight twenty-five
Down to the Rose Bay wharf I drive.
Park my Humber underneath a tree,
Pop along the gangplank and then I'm free.
Free, says you, well how can that be
When you always finish up at Circular Quay?
Oh doubting Tom I shall explain,
When I get on board I sing this sweet refrain:

Chorus:
Where are we going today Mr Nicolson,
Where is it going to be?
Don't turn left, turn right down the
  harbour
And out to the open sea.
Throw away the compass right hand down
And it's out through the heads we'll go,
So oh let's be merry on the Rose Bay·
  ferry,
If we run out of petrol we'll row yo ho,
If we run out of petrol we'll row.

Monday Java, Tuesday Spain,
Wednesday Tokyo and back again.
The only trouble is there isn't any gents,
But what do you want for twenty cents?
Out with me raincoat and me woolly vest,
See the naked ladies on my chest.
Today is Friday so hold on tight
Because it's off to Trinidad and back tonight.

Chorus:
Where are we going today Mr Nicolson,
Where is it going to be?
Don't turn left, turn right down the harbour
And out to the open sea.
Pull up your anchor, pull your finger out
And wave goodbye to your home,
We're off to Nantucket, so give that man a
  bucket
Because it's choppy when you're out on the
  foamy foam,
It's choppy when you're out on the foam.

Now sometimes if I get up late
I only reach the jetty at half past eight,
But that doesn't ruin my world-wide trip
Because the eight thirty-seven is a battleship.
Off on the dot with our guns on high,
Mince up Manly as we pass by,
We need another rocket so just pop upstairs,
You can get them from the chappy who collects the fares.

Chorus:
Where are we going today Mr Nicolson,
Where is it going to be?
Don't turn left, turn right down the harbour
And out to the open sea.
'Cause though we look like dudes and doctors, at heart
We are men of the sea,
So hold on be merry on the Rose Bay ferry
Until we get to Circular Quay you'll see,
We finish up at Circular Quay.

Bernard Bolan

Down Under

*The pop cognoscenti nod knowingly and recall the international success of Colin Hay's
"Down Under" in 1981 when Men at Work first recorded it. But the song was to
become the property of all Australians in 1983 when it was heard as the theme song of
the America's Cup challenge team — and this time Australia was triumphant. The
cognoscenti nod again. Australia's success, they know, is due more to Men at Work's
keening than Lexcen's keeling.*

Travelling in a fried-out Kombi,
On a hippie trail, head full of zombie,
I met a strange lady, she made me nervous,
She took me in and gave me breakfast,
And she said...

"Do you come from a land down under?
Where women glow and men plunder,
Can't you hear, can't you hear the thunder,
You better run, you better take cover."

Buying bread from a man in Brussels,
He was six-foot four and full of muscles,
I said "Do you speak my language?"
He just smiled and gave me a Vegemite sandwich,
And he said...

"I come from a land down under,
Where beer does flow and men chunder,
Can't you hear, can't you hear the thunder,
You better run, you better take cover."

Lying in a den in Bombay,
With a slack jaw and not much to say,
Said to the man "Are you trying to tempt me?
Because I come from the land of plenty?"
And he said...

"Oh! Do you come from a land down under?
Where women glow and men plunder,
Can't you hear, can't you hear the thunder,
You better run, you better take cover."

Colin Hay

TO EARN MY SCREW
AND DO MY DUE

Flash Jack from Gundagai

Banjo Paterson first collected this boastful ballad in his Old Bush Songs *and it is his solutions to the colloquial mysteries that are given here.*
"Wolseleys" and "B-bows" are respectively machines and hand shears, and "pinking" means that the sheep was so closely shorn that the pink skin showed through.
"Whalin' up the Lachlan" was fishing for cod in the river — generally a pursuit of swaggies who'd make their camps by river bends.
To "ring" a shed and "blue" it — "Flash Jack" became the ringer or fastest shearer of the shed and then spent his earnings in a single week's drunken spree.

I've shore at Burrabogie, and I've shore at Toganmain,
I've shore at big Willandra and out on the Coleraine,
But before the shearing was over, I wished myself back again
A-shearing for old Tom Patterson on the One Tree Plain.

Chorus:
All among the wool boys, all among the wool,
Keep your wide blades full boys, keep your wide blades full,
I can do a respectable tally myself, whenever I likes to try,
They know me round the country as Flash Jack from Gundagai.

I've shore at big Willandra and I've shore at Tilberoo,
And once I drew my blades boys upon the famed Barcoo,
At Cowan Downs and Trida, as far as Moulamein,
But I was always glad to get back again to the One Tree Plain.

I've pinked 'em with the Wolseleys and rushed with B-bows too
And shaved 'em in the grease my lads, with the grass seeds showing through,
But I never slummed my pen, my lads, whatever it might contain,
While shearing for old Tom Patterson on the One Tree Plain.

I've been whalin' up the Lachlan, and I've dossed on Cooper's Creek,
And once I rung Cudjingie shed, and I blued it in a week.
But when Gabriel blows his trumpet, I'll catch the morning train,
And push for old Tom Patterson's on the One Tree Plain.

Anon.

The Springtime It Brings On the Shearing

This song was taken from E. J. Overbury's longer poem "On the Wallaby Track", first published in 1865.

The springtime it brings on the shearing,
And it's then you will see them in droves,
To the west-country stations all steering,
A-seeking a job off the coves.

Chorus:
With my raggedy old swag on my shoulder
And a billy quart-pot in my hand,
I tell you we'll 'stonish the new chums,
When they see how we travel the land.

From Boonabri up to the border,
Then it's over to Bourke; there and back.
On the hills and the plains you will see them,
The men on the Wallaby Track.

And after the shearing is over
And the wool season's all at an end,
It is then you will see the flash shearers
Making johnny-cakes round in the bend.

E. J. Overbury

Click Go the Shears

*With the exception of "Waltzing Matilda", this is the best known Australian folksong
and yet, as Bill Scott records in his Australian Folklore, it has gained its popularity
only in the past couple of decades. While the words are homegrown, the tune is an
import from a song called "Ring the Bell Watchman", written by Henry Clay Work,
who still gets international airplay with such ancient chart-toppers as
"Grandfather's Clock" and "Marching through Georgia". For the mystified, "yoe" is a
version of ewe corrupted in the service of rhyme.*

Out on the board the old shearer stands,
Grasping his shears in his thin bony hands;
Fixed is his gaze on a bare-bellied yoe
Glory if he gets her, won't he make the ringer go.

Chorus:
Click go the shears boys, click, click, click,
Wide is his blow and his hands move quick,
The ringer looks around and is beaten by a blow,
And curses the old snagger with the bare-bellied yoe.

In the middle of the floor in his cane-bottomed chair
Sits the boss of the board with his eyes everywhere,
Notes well each fleece as it comes to the screen,
Paying strict attention that it's taken off clean.

The colonial experience man, he is there of course,
With his shiny leggin's on, just got off his horse,
Gazes all around him like a real connoisseur,
Scented soap, and brilliantine and smelling like a whore.

The tar-boy is there waiting in demand
With his blackened tar-pot, in his tarry hand,
Spies one old sheep with a cut upon its back,
Hears what he's waiting for it's "Tar here, Jack!"

Now the shearing is all over, we've all got our cheques
So roll up your swags and it's off down the track.
The first pub we come to it's there we'll have a spree,
And everyone that comes along it's "Have a drink with me."

There we leave him standing shouting for all hands,
Whilst all around him every "shouter" stands,
His eye is on the keg which now is lowering fast,
He works hard, he drinks hard, and goes to hell at last!

Anon.

The Banks of the Condamine

Most folklorists point out the indebtedness of this song to an English ballad "On the Banks of the Nile" — a dialogue between a girl and her soldier lover who was off to fight Napoleon in Egypt. Women will note a theme still current in Australian life — goodness knows how Nancy hoped to prevail over her mate when "the boys are waiting".

Man:
O hark the dogs are barking, love, I can no longer stay;
The men are all gone mustering, and it is nearly day.
And I must be off by morning light before the sun does shine,
To meet the Roma shearers on the banks of the Condamine.

Girl:
O Willy, dearest Willy, O let me go with you!
I'll cut off all my auburn fringe, and be a shearer too;
I'll cook and count your tally, love, while ringer-O you shine,
And I'll wash your greasy moleskins on the banks of the Condamine.

Man:
O Nancy, dearest Nancy, with me you cannot go!
The squatters have given orders, love, no woman should do so.
And your delicate constitution is not equal unto mine,
To withstand the constant tigering on the banks of the Condamine.

Girl:
O Willy, dearest Willy, then stay at home with me;
We'll take up a selection, and a farmer's wife I'll be.
I'll help you husk the corn, love, and cook your meals so fine
You'll forget the ram-stag mutton on the banks of the Condamine.

Man:
O Nancy, dearest Nancy, pray do not hold me back!
Down there the boys are waiting, and I must be on the track.
So here's a goodbye kiss, love; back home I will incline
When we've shore the last of the jumbucks on the banks of the Condamine.

Anon.

Australia Square

"This was the first song that I wrote in Australia," recalls Bernard Bolan, "and I still sing it today. I was at that stage working in the Summit building at Australia Square, and the wonderful sub-culture in our society constituted by the occupants of a high-rise lift seemed ideal material. Funnily enough, the line which runs: 'that silly little bugger from Colonial Sugar...' proved to be prophetic — I went to work for them two years ago. I am thinking of writing a song about being Prime Minister."

Every day I wend my way
To the middle of Sydney town
To earn my screw and do my due
For a company of renown.
I do my chore on the fortieth floor
Of a building round and tall,
Up in the sky where the rents are high
And we all do sweet damn all.

Chorus:
Flash goes the light and ring goes the bell
And up in the air we go,
Sailing in the Summit lift to the land of ice and snow.
Up past the names that we've never heard
Of the people we don't know,
I earn my bread with Sydney spread six hundred feet below.

On the ground floor
Near the big lift door
The crowds all huddle round.
In our castle in the air there's all creeds there
There's yellow, white and brown.
The doors gape wide and we trudge inside
And terror fills the air,
Three, two, one, zero all hope is gone, tell mother I still care.

Chrysler, Wimpey, Esso and Clyde
And old BP and Co.,
The names go past so devilish fast
We must be near the snow.
At thirty-three which is Hitachi,
Seventeen Japanese gold,
And that silly little bugger from Colonial Sugar
Is standing on my toe.

It's strange the way that every day
We trace our heavenly track,
The ones who want to get out first
Are always at the back.
So push the button,
Mind the door, stiffen up your knee,
Sorry miss, I meant to press number forty-three.

Bernard Bolan

31

IT'S OUR HOMELAND

FULL
WORDS
20¢

ALSO
SOUVENIRS
ASHTRAYS
KEYCHAINS

Advance Australia Fair

Until 11 April 1984 this was Australia's national tune only. On that day it became our official national anthem, with both words and music in good odour and in order, except when there's royalty or vice-royalty about. Then "God Save the Queen/King" gets an airing.

Since 1826, apparently, we've been searching for a distinctly Australian song as an anthem. In that year John Dunmore Lang composed two contenders, "The Australian Hymn" and "The Australian Anthem". Among the hundreds of others in the running over the years since then were "The Song of Australia" by Carl Linger and Caroline Carleton, and "Waltzing Matilda". A further inundation of contenders (1300 musical arrangements and 2500 songs) swamped organisers of an official anthem contest in the early 1970s. The eventual choice of "Advance Australia Fair" was as a result of an opinion poll conducted in 1974 and later confirmed by referendum response in 1977.

Australians all let us rejoice,
For we are young and free,
We've golden soil and wealth for toil,
Our home is girt by sea.
Our land abounds in nature's gifts
Of beauty rich and rare,
In history's page let ev'ry stage
Advance Australia Fair.

Beneath our radiant Southern Cross,
We'll toil with hearts and hands,
To make this Commonwealth of ours
Renowned of all the lands;
For those who've come across the seas
We've boundless plains to share
With courage let us all combine
To Advance Australia Fair.

In joyful strains then let us sing
Advance Australia Fair.

P. D. McCormick

God Bless Australia

Jack O'Hagan's answer to the quest for a national anthem — words to stir a chauvinistic soul set to the popular Marie Cowan music for "Waltzing Matilda".

Here in this God given land of ours Australia,
This proud possession, our own piece of earth,
That was built by our fathers, who pioneered our heritage,
Here in Australia, the land of our birth.

Refrain:
God bless Australia, our land Australia,
Home of the Anzac, the strong and the free,
It's our homeland, our own land,
To cherish for eternity,
God bless Australia, the land of the free.

Here in Australia, we treasure love and liberty,
Our way of life, all for one, one for all,
We're a peace-loving race, but should danger ever threaten us,
Let the world know, we will answer the call.

Jack O'Hagan

The Song of Australia

Mrs Caroline Carleton's lyrics and Mr Carl Linger's music won for them the 1859 Gawler Institute National Song Competition. Both were Adelaide-based and the song has an enduring place in the hearts of native-born South Australians. In 1880 the South Australian state government ordered that it be sung in state schools. Without duress, schools in other states followed suit and today primary school pupils throughout the land are quite unfazed by "witching harmonies", "bright vigils" and "mammon's shrine", and thoroughly enjoy its rich turn of phrase.

There is a land where summer skies
Are gleaming with a thousand dyes,
Blending in witching harmonies, in harmonies,
And grassy knoll and forest height
Are flushing in the rosy light,
And all above is azure bright,
Australia, Australia, Australia.

There is a land where honey flows,
Where laughing corn luxuriant grows,
Land of the myrtle and the rose, land of the rose.
On hill and plain the clust'ring vine
Is gushing out with purple wine,
And cups are quaffed to thee and thine,
Australia, Australia, Australia.

There is a land where treasures shine
Deep in the dark unfathomed mine, for
Worshippers at mammon's shrine, at mammon's shrine,
Where gold lies hid, and rubies gleam,
And faded wealth no more doth seem
The idle fancy of a dream,
Australia, Australia, Australia.

There is a land where homesteads peep
From sunny plain and woodland steep, and
Love and joy bright vigils keep, bright vigils keep,
Where the glad voice of childish glee,
Is mingled with the melody,
Of nature's hidden minstrelsy,
Australia, Australia, Australia.

There is a land where floating free,
From mountain top to girding sea,
A proud flag waves exultingly, exultingly,
And Freedom's sons the banner bear,
No shackled slave can breathe the air,
Fairest of Britain's daughters fair,
Australia, Australia, Australia.

C. J. Carleton

My City of Sydney

The music of this serenade was written by American singer Tommy Leonetti for a show in which he appeared on Sydney's Channel 7 in the early 1970s. Channel 7 have used it as a station closer for the past 10 years. Now insomniac Sydneysiders who have been able to hum along to it for the decade can sing along as well.

Natives of intriguing San Francisco,
Surely they can't care if I'm more excited
About her sister city far across the sea.

My city of Sydney I miss the warmth of you,
Miss the heart of your people,
That little church steeple in Woolloomooloo.
Sailboats white polka-dotting the blue of the bay,
As they glide on their way through a clear afternoon,
Night folks thirsting for fun — meeting most ev'ry one,
At the Cross as they toss in their merry balloon.

My city of Sydney I miss your glow at dark,
Miss the Op'ra House lights
From the Bridge, and the nights in a quiet Hyde Park.
Tho' I'm thousands of miles from the surfers
And smiles of your laugh-loving children at play,
My warm city of Sydney I've never been away.

Bobby Troup

Goodbye, Melbourne Town

This short paean to Melbourne, penned in 1934 by a New Zealander and set to music by Australian Fred Hall, is still a popularly requested number from the repertoire of the publishers, Allans Music of Melbourne Town.

Goodbye, Melbourne Town, Melbourne Town, goodbye,
I am leaving you today for a country far away,
Though today I'm stony broke without a single brown,
If I make a fortune I'll come back and spend it in dear old Melbourne town.

Leonard Nelson

Have You Ever Been to See Kings Cross?

Frankie Davidson reveals that this canticle on Sydney's Cross was in fact recorded in Melbourne in April 1963. For the benefit of those who had not been to see Kings Cross pre decimalisation, a "con man's swy" is a double-headed penny used for two-up, a "tenner" is ten pounds and a "zack" is sixpence. Another glimpse of the old Cross is given in the words originally intended for verse two — "Or you could try the Chew and Chunder, you get three courses for a zack". The Chew and Chunder was the name given by patrons with affection, if not complete accuracy, to the worst eating spot in town.

If you think you've done some travelling, like to say you've been around,
That you've seen the sights of Paris or the heart of London Town,
You might say a night in Soho would be mighty hard to toss,
But let me tell you folks that you just ain't lived
Until you've seen Kings Cross.

Chorus:
Have you ever been to see Kings Cross where Sydneysiders meet?
There's a million faces goin' places walkin' up 'n down the street.
Why tourists everywhere in their travels do declare
I've seen the world you can hear 'em cry,
And they'll bet you a tenner to a con man's swy
You won't have seen the lot until the day you die
If you haven't been to see Kings Cross.

Let's take the eating houses that you find along the way,
You might like to dine with a glass of wine or a serve of Shrimp Mornay,
Or you can try the spots down under, you get a three course for a zack,
Where you can write your will as you pay the bill
Just in case you don't get back.

You've got a list of spots to see and you'd like to spend some dough
So you tell the taxi driver just where you'd like to go,
You might do a tour of Sydney when in fact it's on the cards
That the place you sought when you climbed aboard
Was up the road a hundred yards.

So if you're a weary traveller and you think you've seen the lot
Well take my tip and make the trip while the money you've still got,
And in later conversation you'll never be at a loss
'Cos you can tell 'em all that you had a ball
When you went to see Kings Cross.

Frankie Davidson

I Still Call Australia Home

The date: 27 May 1980; the time: late evening; the place: the Sydney Opera House; the crowd, stirred to sartorial splendour by the presence of HM the Queen of Australia: glittering. It was the first time most of the locals had heard this paean to the homeland by a homesick native son. Their appreciative rattling of jewellery thundered through the hall and was echoed by many spellbound viewers of the telecast, in the privacy of their homes. A new national song had been delivered unto us.
"When you write an honest song," Peter has said of it, "you never know what will happen to it."

I've been to cities that never close down,
From New York to Rio and old London town,
But no matter how far or how wide I roam,
I still call Australia home.

Verse:
I'm always trav'lin',
I love being free,
And so I keep leaving the sun and the sea,
But my heart lies waiting — over the foam.
I still call Australia home.

All the sons and daughters spinning 'round the world,
Away from their fam'ly and friends,
But as the world gets older and colder and colder,
It's good to know where your journey ends.

Verse:
But someday we'll all be together once more,
When all of the ships come back to the shore,
I realise something I've always known,
I still call Australia home.

But no matter how far or how wide I roam,
I still call Australia, I still call Australia,
I still call Australia home.

Peter Allen

We Don't Know How Lucky We Are

Written by the inimitable Fred Dagg, "We Don't Know How Lucky We Are" brings a trans-Tasman breadth to this collection. Fred explains that this "is sung to a simple country tune except when performed in Europe when it is sung to Mahler's Ninth, which is a fairly simple country tune submerged in loud, boring, heavy-handed orchestral nonsense. Such a pity really."

I was speaking to a mate of mine
Just the other day,
A guy called Bruce Bayliss, actually,
Who lives up our way.
He's been living in Europe
For the year, more or less;
I says "How was Europe Bruce?"
He says "Fred, it's a mess!

We don't know how lucky we are mate,
We don't know how lucky we are."

My father-in-law has been feeling
Pretty pleased with himself,
He's been living in Greece
For the good of his health,
I said "How was the climate?
And how was your year?"
He says "The climate's too hot,
You can't get a beer,
The sheilas look like blokes
And of course the blokes are all queer."
He says "The Turks and the Arabs
They live far too near,
And if you're going to have a really good
    time,
You might as well live here."

He said "We don't know how lucky we are
    mate",
He says "We don't know how lucky we are."

I was down the "Plough and Cheque Book"
Ooh — night before last,
There's a guy down there on the floor
With his brain at half-mast.
I said "You're looking really bad mate
Your eyes look like string."
He said "Get me an eight will you Fred
    please?
I can't see a thing."

We don't know how lucky we are mate,
We don't know how lucky we are.

There's a mate of mine who lives in town,
I see him about once a year,
He's had a coronary since Easter,
He's got a haemorrhage in his ear,
He went bankrupt a couple of weeks back,
And now his wife's left him too.
I said "You're looking odd mate,
You're looking queer,
What are you going to do?"

He said "We don't know how lucky we are
    mate",
He says "We don't know how lucky we are."

My stock agent's got a beach place
Where he spends most of his days.
His wife bit the dust down there last year,
(Got eaten by a couple of crays),
And his two littlest daughters
Got killed by a whale.
I said "Are you goin' down there this year
    mate?"
He said "Fred — right on the nail!

We don't know how fortunate we are to have
    that place,
We don't know how propitious are the
    circumstances, Frederick."

So when things are looking really bad
And you're thinking of giving it away,
Remember New Zealand's a cracker
And I reckon, come what may,
If things get appallingly bad
And we all get atrociously poor,
If we stand in the queue with our hats on
We can borrow a few million more.

We don't know how lucky we are mate,
We don't know how lucky we are.

We've no idea of the luck we possess,
We just don't know how lucky we all are.

Fred Dagg

Edna's Favourite Things

Two songs from that ambassadress of Australian style, Dame Edna Everage. From the show Excuse I, 1964, *comes "Edna's Favourite Things" and from* Just a Show, 1968, *"Edna's Hymn" which is sung,* con brio, *to the tune of "All Things Bright and Beautiful" (Hymns, Ancient and Modern, no. 573).*
We are deeply indebted to Mr Barry Humphries for providing the following notes to assist the modern reader.
"Edna's Favourite Things"
Mallee root: *an ethnic fuel;* Mr Whippy: *a legendary ice-cream purveyor;* Buckley's Canadiol Mixture: *a popular Australian linctus tested in blizzardly cold Canada;* Maidenhair: *Maidenhair fern, a decorative plant.*
"Edna's Hymn"
A flyaway panel: *a fashion feature of most up-market, Thai-silk ladies' coats in the faraway sixties;* Normie Rowe: *the 1968 equivalent of the 1980s' Peter Allen; the* Little Man who's open round the corner: *invariably an industrious Levantine emigré.*

Recitative:
East, west; home's best,
Distance lends enchantment to a view,
There's no place like home,
Far-off fields are greener —
They're all old sayings, but they are true.
Now, I've seen a lot of things abroad that
   really have dismayed me,
And I wouldn't live in England even if you
   paid me,
For Australia is the only land that's free,
And it's the Little Things in life that appeal to
   me.

Chorus:
A Mallee root glowing on nights when it's
   nippy,
The hushed, muffled music of nice Mr Whippy,
The scratch of hot sand on the seat of the car,
A nice Hoadleys' Violet Crumble Bar,
Blue Hills on the wireless — the perfume of
   Wattle,
The last dregs inside a Tomato Sauce bottle,
Persil suds on your hands when the telephone
   rings —
These are a few of my favourite things.
It's Australia, it's our homeland.
Why not shout it aloud?
You just have to think of your favourite things,
And then you will feel so proud.

I've got a few "musts" in my medicine fixture:
Menthoids and Buckley's Canadiol Mixture,
Dexal, Peroxide, Zinc Cream and Vicks,
Mercalised Wax and Syrup of Figs,
Smellings Salts by Yardley for times of
   emotion,
Milk of Magnesia and Calomine Lotion,

Citronella to ward off the old mozzie stings —
These are a few of my favourite things.

Lamingtons, Drop Scones and Vanilla Slices,
Cream Puffs, and Apple Cakes dusted with
   spices,
Apricot Swiss Roll and chewy Hedgehog,
Banana Pavlova and Chocolate Log,
A plate of Iced Vovos so moist and enticing,
A lovely Cream Sponge Cake with Passionfruit
   icing,
And Butterfly Cakes with their little sponge
   wings —
These are a few of my favourite things.
It's Australia, it's our homeland.
Why not shout it aloud?
You just have to think of your favourite things,
And then you will feel so proud.

White Cabbage Moths round Tomato Plants
   flitting,
The swish of a Sprinkler, the smell of new
   Knitting,
Tea leaves on the Maidenhair — Silverfish in
   the bath,
The Sugar Ants' trail up my Front Cement
   Path,
Snails in the letter box — Moths in the lamp,
The design for our latest Australian Stamp,
And those glamorous things that the Avon
   Lass brings:
These are a few of my favourite things.
It's Australia, it's our homeland.
Why not shout it aloud?
You just have to think of your favourite things,
And then you will feel so proud.

Barry Humphries

Edna's Hymn

Recitative:
When I get home from a day's shopping in a city street,
I pop on the kettle, though I'm nearly dropping on my feet —
Make a nice cup of tea.
Then I switch on my favourite channel,
It's the best time for me as I flick off my flyaway panel.
When I get home from a treat at a flesh-and-blood theatre —
If you call it a treat peering up and down each street for a meter —
I think of old songs and the memories they bring back,
While my thoughtful Norm helps me off with my left and right sling-back.
And I think of old songs from old shows as I powder my nose,
And I think of a dear old hymn that time will never dim for me —
Before I met my Norm it was the only hymn for me.

Chorus:
All things bright and beautiful, all creatures great and small,
All things wise and wonderful, Australia has them all:
Our famous ballerinas, Joan Sutherland their star,
Our Hoover vacuum cleaners, our Cadbury's chocolate bar,
A cloth all Persil snowy for Austral picnic spread,
Where hums the humble blowie and beetroot stains the bread.

All things bright and beautiful — Pavlovas that we bake,
All things wise and wonderful — Australia takes the cake.
Our great big smiling beaches, the smell of thick Kwik Tan,
Our lovely juicy peaches that never blow the can,
Our gorgeous modern cities so famed throughout the earth,
The Paris end of Collins Street, the Melbourne end of Perth.

All things bright and beautiful — though cynics sneer and plot,
All things wise and wonderful — Australia's got the lot!
The Farex that we scrape off those wee Australian chins,
The phenol that we sprinkle inside our rubbish bins,
Our plate-glass picture windows, venetians open wide —
In the land where nothing happens, there's nothing much to hide.

All things bright and beautiful —
Our wonderful wealth of natural mineral resources.
All things wise and wonderful —
And our even more wonderful wealth of different brands of tomato sauces.

Coda:
Australia is a Saturday with races on the trannie;
Australia is the talcy smell of someone else's granny;
Australia is a kiddie with zinc cream on its nose;
Australia's voice is Melba's voice — it's also Normie Rowe's;
Australia's famous postage stamps are stuffed with flowers and fauna;
Australia is the Little Man who's open round the corner.
Australia is a sunburnt land of sand and surf and snow;
All ye who do not love her — ye know where ye can go.

Barry Humphries

DIGGER WAS A SOLDIER

Mademoiselle from Armentieres

One of the classic soldier songs from World War I, this printable version appeared in Digger Aussiosities *printed in Sydney in the 1920s.*

"Mademoiselle from Armentieres,
Parley-voo!"
Sang the Diggers between their beers,
Parley-voo!
And the ballad roared by the soldiers gay,
Rang through the old estaminet —
"Inky-pinky, parley-voo!"
Mademoiselle enjoyed the din,
Parley-voo!
As she tripped around with the *bock* and *vin,*
Parley-voo!
And *Mademoiselle,* in a manner gay,
Trolled a stave of the ribald lay —
"Inky-pinky, parley-voo!"
There were men from Wagga and Gundagai,
Parley-voo!
From Perth, and The Towers, and Boggabri,
Parley-voo!
From Sydney City and Dandenong,
Sinking their troubles in wine and song —
Inky-pinky, parley-voo!
There was one young Digger, tanned and lean,
Parley-voo!
From Darling Downs, or the Riverine,
Parley-voo!

Who set her heart in a rapturous whirl
When he vowed that she was his Dinkum Girl —
Inky-pinky, parley-voo!
They laughed and loved in the old French town,
Parley-voo!
And her heart spake out of her eyes of brown,
Parley-voo!
But the time fled by, and there came a day
When he and his cobbers all marched away —
Inky-pinky, parley-voo!
Maybe on a field of France he fell,
Parley-voo!
No word came back to *Mademoiselle,*
Parley-voo!
But a pretty French girl, with eyes of brown,
Prays for him still in a war-swept town,
Inky-pinky, parley-voo!
Quiet the old estaminet,
Parley-voo!
No more Diggers will come that way,
Parley-voo!
May your heart grow light with the passing years,
Oh, *Mademoiselle* from Armentieres! —
Inky-pinky, parley-voo!

Anon.

I'm Going Back to Yarrawonga

There were a few World War I songs that all the family could sing. A more decorous if idealistic note is struck in Neil McBeath's "Yarrawonga" — where the skies are always blue.

Now Digger was a soldier, and he sailed across the sea
With the first Anzac Brigade,
And Digger was a soldier as brave as one could be,
And a grand old name he's made.
From the landing at Gallipoli till the war clouds left the skies
He wandered round the Continent, a tourist in disguise,
Then after years of battling, when three parts full of lead,
The MO said, "We'll send you home": 'twas then old Digger said,

Chorus:
"I'm going back again to Yarrawonga,
In Yarrawonga I'll linger longer,
I'm going back again to Yarrawonga,
Where the skies are always blue,
And when I'm back again in Yarrawonga
I'll soon be stronger than old Mahonga.
You can have all your Tennessee and Caroline,
France and Belgium thrown in, take the whole lot for mine.
I'm going back again to Yarrawonga
And the land of the Kangaroo."

Now Digger was a soldier, so he went back home again
In the good ship Majarine,
And Digger was a soldier, he couldn't settle down,
For a dinkum Anzac he'd been.
He daily read the papers of doings at the front,
Of all the latest victories and every blooming stunt.
One day he re-enlisted, he did without a doubt,
And out in France when peace had come again they heard him shout,

Neil McBeath

47

Dinky Di

A few of the cleaner verses from this popular World War 1 song. The song is sometimes called "Horseferry Road" which was the address of Australian Army Headquarters in London.

He came over to London and straight away strode,
To army headquarters in Horseferry Road,
To see all the bludgers who dodge all the strafe,
By getting soft jobs on the headquarters staff.
Dinky di, dinky di,
By getting soft jobs on the headquarters staff.

A lousy lance-corporal said, "Pardon me, please,
You've mud on your tunic and blood on your sleeve,
You look so disgraceful the people will laugh,"
Said the lousy lance-corporal on the headquarters staff.
Dinky di, dinky di,
Said the lousy lance-corporal on the headquarters staff.

The digger then shot him a murderous glance;
He said: "We're just back from the balls-up in France,
Where bullets are flying and comforts are few,
And brave men are dying for bastards like you;
Dinky di, dinky di,
And brave men are dying for bastards like you."

"We're shelled on the left and we're shelled on the right,
We're bombed all the day and we're bombed all the night,
And if something don't happen, and that pretty soon,
There'll be nobody left in the bloody platoon;
Dinky di, dinky di,
There'll be nobody left in the bloody platoon."

This story soon got to the ears of Lord Gort,
Who gave the whole matter a great deal of thought,
He awarded the digger a VC and two bars,
For giving that corporal a kick up the arse;
Dinky di, dinky di,
For giving that corporal a kick up the arse.

Now when this war's over and we're out of here,
We'll see him in Sydney town begging for beer.
He'll ask for a dina to buy a small glass,
But all he'll get is a kick in the arse.

Anon.

48

The Band Played Waltzing Matilda

Eric Bogle writes: "The Band Played Waltzing Matilda was written in Canberra in 1972 shortly after I had witnessed my first Anzac Day march. Like all similar marches, remembrance days, wreath layings etc., I found it a bit pointless and pathetic, but strangely moving, especially seeing the old 'Diggers', some of whom could barely walk, trying to recapture the swank and discipline of 60 years ago, swinging along valiantly trying to march in step, denying arthritis, old age and tired old bones. It was sobering to watch the young present-day soldiers side by side with the old veterans, and reflect on the procession of wars, suffering and death that were represented by the three different generations of soldiers in that Anzac Day march. I wrote the song for two main reasons — as my own personal anti-war statement and as a tribute to the Diggers of Gallipoli. It is, I hope, an honest and restrained comment on war. I would point out that the song contains a couple of historical inaccuracies. I was aware of that when I wrote it but I wanted to communicate feelings, emotion, and I believe history is the preserve of the historians, not poets. However, I make no apologies for anything contained in the song. I believed in everything I wrote then, and believe in it still."

When I was a young man I carried a pack
And I lived the free life of a rover,
From the Murray's green banks to the
    dusty outback,
I waltzed my Matilda all over.
Then in 1915, the country said, "Son,
There's no time for rovin', there's work to
    be done,"
And they gave me a tin hat, and gave me
    a gun,
And they sent me away to the war.

Chorus:
And the band played "Waltzing Matilda",
As our ship pulled away from the quay
And amidst all the cheers, the flag-waving
    and tears
We sailed off for Gallipoli.

How well I remember that terrible day,
How the blood stained the sand and the
    water,
And how in that hell that they called
    Suvla Bay
We were butchered like lambs to the
    slaughter;
Johnny Turk he was waiting, he'd primed
    himself well,
He rained us with bullets and showered
    us with shells,
And in ten minutes flat he'd blown us all
    to hell,
Nearly blew us right back to Australia.

Chorus:
But the band played "Waltzing Matilda",
When we stopped to bury the slain,
We buried ours, and the Turks buried
    theirs,
Then we started all over again.

And those that were left, well, we tried to
survive
In a mad world of death, blood and fire,
And for nearly ten weeks I kept myself
alive,
Though around me the corpses piled
higher;
Then a big Turkish shell knocked me arse
over head,
And when I woke up in my hospital bed
I saw what it had done, and I wished I
was dead,
Never knew there were worse things than
dying.

Chorus:
For I'll go no more waltzing Matilda
All around the wild bush far and free,
To hump tent and pegs, a man needs
both legs,
No more waltzing Matilda for me.

Then they gathered the sick and the
crippled and maimed,
And sent us back home to Australia,
The armless, the legless, the blind and
insane,
The brave wounded heroes of Suvla;
And when our ship pulled into Circular
Quay
I looked at the stumps where my legs used
to be,
And thanked Christ there was nobody
waiting for me
To grieve, to mourn and to pity.

Chorus:
And the band played "Waltzing Matilda"
As they carried us down the gangway,
But nobody cheered, they just stood there
and stared,
Then they turned their faces away.

So every April my old comrades march,
Reviving old dreams and past glory,
And I push my wheelchair out onto the
porch
And watch the parade pass before me;
The old men march slowly, old bones
stiff and sore,
Tired old men from a forgotten war,
The young people ask: "What are they
marching for?"
I ask myself the same question.

Chorus:
And the band plays "Waltzing Matilda",
The old men respond to the call,
But as year follows year, more old men
disappear,
Someday no-one will march there at all.

Coda:
(Use last verse and tune of "Waltzing
Matilda.")

Eric Bogle

THE JOLLY,
JOLLY GROG

All for Me Grog

*First collected by Banjo Paterson, the song describes the hazard known as "lambing
down" practised by publicans and the owners of illegal grog shanties to deprive bushmen
of their hard-won wages. The thirsty bushie would be served alcohol drugged, often with
tobacco. When he woke, hours later, he'd be told how he'd shouted the bar and all there
was to show for his wages was a hangover and the horrors.*
*Kenneth Cook's modern re-working of this sad old tale, Wake in Fright, is truly chilling.
With its fine rollicking tune, a descendant of an early sea song, the ballad is a little easier to bear.*

Well I am a ramblin' lad, and me story it is sad,
If ever I get to Lachlan I should wonder,
For I spent all me brass in the bottom of the glass,
And across the western plains I must wander.

Chorus:
And it's all for me grog, me jolly, jolly grog,
It's all for me beer and tobacco,
For I spent all me tin in a shanty drinking gin,
Now across the western plains I must wander.

Well I'm stiff, stony broke and I've parted from me moke,
And the sky is lookin' back as flamin' thunder;
The shanty boss is blue 'cause I haven't got a sou,
That's the way they treat you when you're down and under.

I'm crook in the head and I haven't been to bed,
Since first I touched this shanty with me plunder.
I see centipedes and snakes, and I'm full of aches and shakes,
And I think it's time to push for way out yonder.

I'll take to the Old Man Plain, and criss-cross him once again,
Until me eyes the track no longer see, boys;
And me beer and whisky brain search for sleep, but all in vain,
And I feel as if I've had the Darling Pea, boys.

So it's hang yer jolly grog, yer hocussed shanty grog,
The beer that is loaded with tobacco;
Graftin' humour I am in, and I'll stick the peg right in
And settle down once more to some hard yakka.

Anon.

The Old Keg of Rum

In some quarters it will be argued that it is every Australian's duty to keep alive by imitation the fine practices of colonial life. Those who linger round the keg at the club barbie have doubtless painstakingly researched their subject and deserve our thanks for their selfless devotion to the preservation of so excellent a tradition.

My name is old Jack Palmer,
I'm a man of olden days,
And so I wish to sing a song
To you of olden praise;
To tell of merry friends of old
When we were gay and young;
How we sat and sang together
Round the Old Keg of Rum.

Chorus:
Oh! the Old Keg of Rum! the Old Keg of Rum!
How we sat and sang together
Round the Old Keg of Rum.

There was I and Jack the ploughboy,
Jem Moore and old Tom Hines,
And poor old Tom the fiddler,
Who now in glory shines;
And several more of our old chums,
Who shine in Kingdom Come,
We all associated round the
Old Keg of Rum.

Chorus:
Oh! the Old Keg of Rum! the Old Keg of Rum!
We all associated round the
Old Keg of Rum.

And when harvest time was over,
And we'd get our harvest fee,
We'd meet, and quickly rise the keg,
And then we'd have a spree.
We'd sit and sing together
Till we got that blind and dumb
That we couldn't find the bunghole
Of the Old Keg of Rum.

Chorus:
Oh! the Old Keg of Rum! the Old Keg of Rum!
That we couldn't find the bunghole
Of the Old Keg of Rum.

It's jovially together, boys —
We'd laugh, we'd chat, we'd sing;
Sometimes we'd have a little row
Some argument would bring.
And oft-times in a scrimmage, boys,
I've corked it with my thumb,
To keep the life from leaking
From the Old Keg of Rum.

Chorus:
Oh! the Old Keg of Rum! the Old Keg of Rum!
To keep the life from leaking
From the Old Keg of Rum.

But when our spree was ended, boys,
And waking from a snooze,
For to give another dram
The old keg would refuse.
We'd rap it with our knuckles —
If it sounded like a drum,
We'd know the life and spirit
Had left the Old Keg of Rum.

Chorus:
Oh! the Old Keg of Rum! the Old Keg of Rum!
We'd know the life and spirit
Had left the Old Keg of Rum.

Those happy days have passed away,
I've seen their pleasures fade;
And many of our good old friends
Have with old times decayed.
But still, when on my travels, boys,
If I meet with an old chum,
We will sigh, in conversation,
Of the Grand Old Keg of Rum.

Chorus:
Oh! the Old Keg of Rum! the Old Keg of Rum!
We will sigh, in conversation,
Of the Grand Old Keg of Rum.

Anon.

A Pub with No Beer

Inspired by Dan Shean's poem "Pub Without Beer", Gordon Parsons' adaptation of the legend has itself become legendary. In 1958 drinkers at the pub at Taylor's Arm about 30 kilometres from Kalang, Gordon's home town, could recognise themselves among the verses. "The pub is still there," Gordon reports, "and we have a Pub With No Beer Festival every Easter, when about 10,000 people join in." Does the beer run out? we ask.

It's lonesome away from your kindred and all,
By the campfire at night where the wild dingoes call,
But there's nothing so lonesome, so morbid or drear
Than to stand in a bar of a pub with no beer!

Now the publican's anxious for the quota to come,
There's a far-away look on the face of the "bum",
The maid's gone all cranky and the cook's acting queer,
What a terrible place is a pub with no beer!

Then the stockman rides up with his dry dusty throat,
He breasts up to the bar, pulls a wad from his coat,
But the smile on his face quickly turns to a sneer
When the barman says sadly "The pub's got no beer!"

Then the swaggie comes in smother'd in dust and flies,
He throws down his roll, rubs the sweat from his eyes,
But when he is told he says "What's this I hear?
(Spoken)
I've trudged fifty flamin' miles to a pub with no beer!"

There's a dog on the v'randah, for his master he waits,
But the boss is inside drinking wine with his mates,
He hurries for cover and he cringes in fear,
It's no place for a dog round a pub with no beer!

Old Billy the blacksmith the first time in his life
Has gone home cold sober to his darling wife,
He walks in the kitchen, she says "You're early my dear,"
But he breaks down and tells her "The pub's got no beer!"

Gordon Parsons

Duncan

Pat Alexander writes: "In 1974 I was desperately trying to sell an insurance policy to Duncan, the owner of a heat-treatment business at St Peters, Sydney. I called on him four times and on each occasion we finished up at the Town and Country Hotel, just around the corner from the factory. The song came from nowhere as I made my way home from one of these jovial sessions. But it was six years later that the big break came when Slim Dusty recorded 'Duncan' at EMI in Sydney on 15 October 1980. The song captures the indefinable mateship that is essentially Australian. Incidentally, my mate Duncan never did buy an insurance policy."

I love to have a beer with Duncan,
I love to have a beer with Dunc,
We drink in moderation
And we never, ever, ever get rolling drunk.
We drink at the "Town and Country"
Where the atmosphere is great,
I love to have a beer with Duncan
'Cause Duncan's me mate. Yeah!

I love to have a beer with Colin,
I love to have a beer with Col,
We drink in moderation
And it doesn't really matter if he brings his doll.
We drink at the "Town and Country"
Where the atmosphere is great,
I love to have a beer with Colin
'Cause Colin's me mate.

I love to have a beer with Kevin, oh
I love to have a beer with Kev,
We drink in moderation
And he drives me home in the big old Chev.
We drink at the "Town and Country"
Where the atmosphere is great,
I love to have a beer with Kevin
'Cause Kevin's me mate.

I love to have a beer with Patrick,
I love to have a beer with Pat,
We drink in moderation
And it wouldn't really matter if the beer was flat.
We drink at the "Town and Country"
Where the atmosphere is great,
I love to have a beer with Patrick
'Cause Patrick's me mate.

I love to have a beer with Robert,
I love to have a beer with Bob,
We drink in moderation
Just one more and back on the job.
We drink at the "Town and Country"
Where the atmosphere is great,
I love to have a beer with Robert
'Cause Robert's me mate.

I love to have a beer with Duncan, oh
I love to have a beer with Dunc,
We drink in moderation
And we never, ever, ever get rolling drunk.
We drink at the "Town and Country"
Where the atmosphere is great,
I love to have a beer with Duncan
'Cause Duncan's me mate.

Pat Alexander

The Old Pacific Sea

In 1963, Barry Humphries, in the impenetrable guise of an Earl's Court dweller,
composed and recorded this song for Private Eye, London. It was later incorporated into
stage performances and appropriated by fellow expatriate Barry McKenzie. "With its
pioneering references to tubes and ice-cold tinnies," he records, "it extolled for the first
time in the History of the Race the pleasures of chundering."
Sung to the traditional tune of "Maggie May", no serious collection of folklore would be
complete without its inclusion.

Oh, I was down by Bondi pier
Drinking tubes of ice-cold beer
With a bucket full of prawns upon me knee.
But when I'd swallowed the last prawn
I had a Technicolor yawn
And I chundered in the old Pacific sea.

Drink it up. Drink it up.
Crack another dozen tubes and prawns with me.
If you want to throw your voice
Mate, you won't have any choice
But to chunder in the old Pacific sea.

I was sitting in the surf
When a mate of mine called Murph
Asked if he could crack a tube or two with me.
The bastard barely swallowed it
When he went for the big spit
And he chundered in the old Pacific sea.

I've had liquid laughs in bars
And I've hurled from moving cars
And I've chuckled when and where it suited me.
But, if I could choose a spot
To regurgitate me lot
Then I'd chunder in the old Pacific sea.

Barry Humphries

I Feel Like a Tooheys

"Beer," wrote Henry Lawson, "makes you feel the way you ought to feel without beer."
And another Australian poet, sadly anonymous, has written:

Beer, Beer, I love thee;
In thee I place my trust.
I'd rather go to bed with hunger
Than go to bed with thirst.

To which the poets at Mojo Australia have added the following:

How d'ya feel when you walk on the field knowing you're the last to play?
How d'ya feel when you face a new ball and the win is just five runs
    away?
How d'ya feel when you hear the appeal and the umpire says "No way"?
How d'ya feel on the very last ball and only a six will save the day?
How d'ya feel when the ball leaves the field and clears the pickets on the
    way?
How d'ya feel, how d'ya feel?

Chorus:
I feel like a Tooheys, I feel like a Tooheys, I feel like a Tooheys or two,
I feel like a Tooheys, I feel like a Tooheys, I feel like a Tooheys draught brew.

How d'ya feel? Three days at the wheel takin' on the sea and sun.
How d'ya feel? Workin' ropes and steel and there's no rest for anyone.
How d'ya feel when they ride on their keel as if the race had just begun?
How d'ya feel when the spinnaker fills and you're flyin' high on a winning
    run?
How d'ya feel when the gun and the cheers tell you you're first home?
How d'ya feel, how d'ya feel?

How d'ya feel? Manly and the Eels and no-one's givin' an inch today.
How d'ya feel when you dive for his heels too late and the skipper's havin'
    his say?
How d'ya feel? A wall of the Eagles holdin' you back and time's tickin'
    away.
How d'ya feel when you make the call and you've got the ball? Can you save
    the day?
How d'ya feel when you beat them all and they're shoutin' out your
    name?
How d'ya feel, how d'ya feel?

How d'ya feel? Big ride today, it's all T.J., and the money's on.
How d'ya feel? The line-up's right, all is quiet, then the gates are sprung.
How d'ya feel? Way back in the field and only the straight to run.
How d'ya feel as you urge him on, thund'rin' down the last furlong?
How d'ya feel ridin' hands and heels and you know you've got 'em done?
How d'ya feel, how d'ya feel?

How d'ya feel? As you leap in the boat with your heart in your throat and
    grab the oars?
How d'ya feel? Every bone shakes as you smash through the break that is
    like a wall.
How d'ya feel? The boat is soarin' but the sweep is roarin' — he still wants
    more.
How d'ya feel? First round the buoy but you feel no joy, you've lost from
    here before.
How d'ya feel when you crack a wave and you're screamin' for the shore?
How d'ya feel, how d'ya feel?

Mojo Australia

The Butcher's Ballad

An invaluable addition collected by our illustrator whilst OS. Patrick notes: "This
vigorous and traditional affirmation of national identity may be heard wherever
Australians forgather. It was heard by me on the Acropolis at midnight, beneath a
classical moon. That rendition was provided by three butcher's apprentices from Broken
Hill, fresh from the running of the bulls at Pamplona — where they had upset the locals
by wrestling the steer to the ground — and with the mud still between their toes to
prove it."

Miller's Ale and Foster's Lager —
In a bottle or a glass,
It's the health food of a nation;
Stick your ice-cream up your arse.

Anon.

IT'S ALL ABOUT A GIRL

Botany Bay Courtship

*Though possibly not as well-known as other songs in this collection, this lay of the 1830s
has been included to give an introductory example of how the course of true love never
did run smooth in this outpost of empire. Later romantic outpourings seem no less
trouble-free. Sing it, if you can, to the tune of "The Irish Washerwoman".*

The Currency Lads may fill their glasses,
And drink the health of the Currency Lasses,
But the lass I adore, the lass for me,
Is the lass in the Female Factory.

O! Molly's her name, and her name is Molly,
Although she was tried by the name of Polly;
She was tried and sent for death at Newry,
But the judge was bribed and so were the jury.

She got "death recorded" in Newry town
For stealing her mistress's watch and gown;
Her little boy Paddy can tell you the tale,
His father was turnkey at Newry jail.

The first time I saw the comely lass
Was at Parramatta, going to Mass;
Says I: "I'll marry you now in an hour."
Says she: "Well, go and fetch Father Power."

But I got into trouble that very same night!
Being drunk in the street I got into a fight;
A constable seized me — I gave him a box —
And was put in the watch-house and then in
  the stocks.

O! It's very unaisy as I remember,
To sit in the stocks in the month of December,
With the north wind so hot, and the hot sun
  right over,

O! sure, and it's no place at all for a lover!

"It's worse than the treadmill," says I,
  "Mr Dunn,
To sit here all day in the heat of the sun."
"Either that or a dollar," says he, "for your
  folly" —
But if I had a dollar I'd drink it with Molly.

But now I am out again, early and late
I sigh and I cry at the Factory gate.
"O! Mrs Reordan, late Mrs Farson,
O! won't you let Molly out very soon?"

"Is it Molly McGuigan?" says she to me.
"Is it now?" says I, for I know'd it was she.
"Is it her you mean that was put in the stocks
For beating her mistress, Mrs Cox?"

"O! yes and it is, madam, pray let me in,
I have brought her a half-pint of Cooper's
  best gin.
She likes it as well as she likes her own
  mother,
O! now let me in, madam, I am her brother."

So the Currency Lads may fill their glasses,
And drink the health of the Currency Lasses,
But the lass I adore, the lass for me,
Is the lass in the Female Factory.

Anon.

64

Bourke Street on Saturday Night

In its use of the vernacular, its setting and its hero's name, this serenade written by P. C. Cole in 1918 owes much to C. J. Dennis's evergreen Songs of a Sentimental Bloke which was published three years earlier. The music for "Billo", as the song was originally titled, was by Fred Hall whose penchant for the parochial is also expressed in "Goodbye, Melbourne Town".

Them ragtime songs makes me fair pippy,
All Hiwai or old Dixie land
And the same sort av tarts alwuz in 'em
With gold 'air, starry eyes, lily 'ands.
Bah, tell me what's wrong with Orstralia,
An' the clina on which I am shook,
I don't want no cotton fields shady
An' I don't want no soft purlin' brook.

Chorus:
Gimme old Melbourne, an gimme me tart:
An' then I am simply orlright,
Can any bloke point to a better old joint,
Than Bourke Street on Saturday night.
When me an' me Maudie is strolling along
Me cobbers orl try to be smart,
"Git out of ther way, that's Billo", they say,
"Walkin' out with 'is fair dinkum tart".

On Princes Bridge once we wuz standin'
An' gazed at the water below
In the lamplight we feels sentimental
'Oldin' 'ands, all that rot well you know,
Sez Maud "Prove you're fond o' me reely",
So I looks to see no one wuz near.
Then gives 'er a kiss, and she murmurs,
"Now yer loves me I know, Billo dear".

P. C. Cole

Where the Dog Sits on the Tucker Box

First heard in 1928 this song, sometimes called "Five Miles from Gundagai" has retained much of its early popularity. It is Jack O'Hagan's sprightly tune that lights the comfortable vision of true love from Shakespeare's rival "Alf".

I'm just a love-lorn weary coot and I've composed a song,
It's all about a girl I love and dream of all day long —
The rhythm seemed to come to me whilst milking fav'rite cow —
And as my hands went up and down I wrote this song I vow.

Refrain:
My Mabel waits for me underneath the bright blue sky,
Where the dogs sits on the tucker box five miles from Gundagai —
I meet her every day and I know she's dinky di —
Where the dog sits on the tucker box five miles from Gundagai.

Now poets in the days gone by were often much inspired
By lovely wenches that they loved and otherwise admired.
But though they wrote some lovely prose whilst in a state of bliss,
Why even Shakespeare never wrote a poem as good as this.

"Alf"

Is 'E an Aussie?

A jaunty air, tongue-tangling lyrics. There is little surprise that this was written by an old vaudevillian — B. C. Hilliam, Flotsam of the double act Flotsam and Jetsam.

Learn how Lizzie met an Aussie,
Told her girlfriend Mary Ann,
"Mary Ann, I've met a man who
Says he's an Australian."
"Fallen for 'im 'ave you Lizzie?"
Lizzie coyly shook her head,
But Mary Ann knew better than
Believe her pal and said —

Chorus:
"Is 'e an Aussie, is 'e Lizzie?
Is 'e an Aussie is 'e eh?
Is it because 'e is an Aussie that
'E keeps you busy, Lizzie?
'As 'e jazzy ways and does 'e
Make you go all fuzzy wuzzy?
Got you dizzy 'as 'e Lizzie?
Is 'e an Aussie is 'e eh?"

"Seems this Digger likes my figger,"
Lizzie then told Mary Ann.
"Likes my ways and seems to think 'em
What Australians call fair dinkum!
Talks of Bondi, throws a fond eye,
And is teaching me to say 'Good-oh!'"
Said Mary Ann, "My, what a man!
But what I want to know is —

Soon this wonder from Down Under
Got himself right down to biz,
Went on bended knee to Liz and
She said she would be his.
He, being well-born came from Melbourne,
So they sailed at once for there.
Poor Mary Ann without a man,
Repeats her maiden's prayer —

B. C. Hilliam

Silver City Birthday Celebration Day

Brian Cadd recalls putting this song together:
"We recorded the music track for the song very late one night without my having any
lyric idea at all. In order to guide the band along a bit I sort-of mumbled a 'rough'
vocal, making up anything that came into my head. Fortunately it was recorded as well
and listening back to our efforts I discovered that there were lots of 'silver city' and
'silver sequins'-type phrases repeated throughout. Gradually the pictures came to me and
I was able to finish the lyric. My Silver City was entirely fictional! It wasn't until a year
or so later when we played Broken Hill and they made a bit of a fuss over the song did I
tie up Silver City to Broken Hill."

Move it over soldier, let me stand there over by the cider keg,
Let me eat my heart out as we both survey that sweet lady's leg.
Five'll get you ten I'm not the man I'm always tellin' you I'll be,
If she moves a little closer then we'll know which one of us it's gonna be.

Chorus:
Silver City Birthday Celebration Day,
Silver sequins flashing, hope they're goin' my way.
Maybe if I talk to her then she'll want to stay,
Help me to enjoy the Silver City Birthday Celebration Day.

It's the judging of the crochet in the centre ring, I hope my Ma does well,
Or if you want a little laugh we'll go and watch the lady wrestlers for a spell.
I know it's not much fun just standin' round and only drinkin' to stay high,
But if we get ourselves some ladies then hold onto your head we're gonna fly.

Brian Cadd

Howzat

Garth Porter, keyboard player with the group Sherbert who made "Howzat" the popular
success of the 1970s, says of the song: "I guess it's the catchy melody and title that
people connect with. It's one of the worst lyrics I've ever written."
So! Maybe it won't cause A. D. Hope or Judith Wright too much worry about their
laureateships, but it does mark a start. Australians could write, record and perform
popular songs that would be enjoyed all over the world. Such was Sherbert's success with
"Howzat".

You told me I was the one,
The only one who got your head undone,
And for a while I believed the line that you spun.

But I've been lookin' at you,
Lookin' closely at the things you do,
I didn't see you the way you wanted me to.
How, how, howzat?

Chorus:
You messed about, I caught you out, howzat?
Now that I've found where you're at,
It's goodbye,
Well, howzat? It's good-bye.

Oh yeah —

You only came for a smile,
Even though you're really not my style.
I didn't think that you'd run me round like you do.
How, howzat?

Garth Porter and Tony Mitchell

The Newcastle Song

Bob Hudson cryptically explains: "The essence of the 'Newcastle Song' (as published) is that it is the essence of the 'Newcastle Song'. The record you heard was never the record as recorded." Originally recorded, Norm and his buddies cruised the Newcastle streets in their hot FJ Holden for well over 12 minutes. In live performances these days they rival Don Giovanni in his pursuit of a well-turned ankle, taking at least 40 melodious minutes to suss out the action. What we present here is merely the smash-hit edited version — used for the single of the 1970s. This record introduced Hudson's insouciant wit to a wider audience and created a new prosperity in milk bars the length of Hunter Street, Newcastle.

Chorus:
Don't you ever let a chance go by, oh Lord,
Don't you ever let a chance go by.

Yes, up in Newcastle they have very strange mating habits. All the young women of Newcastle walk down the main street which is called Hunter Street for reasons that will become obvious later on in the song. All the young men of Newcastle drive down Hunter Street in their hot FJ Holdens with chrome-plated grease nipples and double reverse overhead twin-cam door handles, sitting eight abreast in the front seat, and they lean out of the window and say real cool things to the sheilas on the footpath, like: "Aah g'day." And every now and then of course one of the young ladies thinks to herself: "Ummmm," she thinks, "Ummmmm."

Chorus:
Don't you ever let a chance go by, oh Lord,
Don't you ever let a chance go by.

Anyway there was this mob of blokes driving down Hunter Street in the front seat of the hot FJ with chrome-plated grease nipples and twin overhead fox tails, and the coolest of them all, who got to sit near the window, was young Norm. And they pulled up outside the Parthenon milk bar and standing outside the Parthenon was this beautiful looking sheila.

"Oooh! Ooooh!" said young Normie, who'd come top in his class in English, "Ooooh!" he said. So he leaned out the window and he said, real, real suave-like, he said: "G'day."

This nine-foot-tall Hell's Angel came out of the Parthenon milk bar, looked at Norm and said: "Arr, what are ya?"

Norm said: "What are you?"

Bloke on the footpath said: "D'ya want a go, do ya mate, eh?"

Norm said: "Yeah, d'you want a go, mate?"

Bloke on the footpath said: "Yeah, I'll have a go."

Norm said: "D'you know who you're picking?"

The bloke on the footpath said: "Nah, who am I picking?"

Norm said: "You find out!" And all of a sudden there was a break in the traffic, and as any young Newcastle lad knows — when you're getting monstered by a nine-foot-tall Hell's Angel and there's a break in the traffic, —

Chorus:
Don't you ever let a chance go by, oh Lord,
Don't you ever let a chance go by.

Bob Hudson and Neville Cruse

Rack Off Normie

*With the success of "The Newcastle Song", the recording company had what Bob and
his collaborator Chris Neal described as "a dreadful idea". They wanted to record an
answer to Normie. So dreadful did Bob and Chris deem this idea that they sat down and
in half an hour had dashed off "the silliest answer song". This, they thought, trusting in
the good taste of the public, would be rejected as too silly. As it turned out, Bob admits,
"Rack Off Normie" "was so silly that it was a lot of fun".*

I was mindin' me business down in the street,
There was a nice Hell's Angel I was hopin' to meet.
I was standin' on the footpath, havin' a nice dream
And he was in the Parthenon, buyin' an ice cream.
Along came a lair in a hot FJ,
He leaned out the window and he said gidday,
He said: "My name's Normie, do you wanna ride?"
And then me Hell's Angel hero came out from inside
He said:

"Rack off, Normie, you and your mates,
I know what you're after, but I'll put you straight.
I'll smash your back window with a great lump of rock,
So rack off now before I do me block, rack off now before I do me
    block" (and they did).

Well that was the last we saw of Norm and the gang,
They shot off up the road with a clatter and bang,
And I said to meself as I walked back inside,
These local blokes here have sure got a hide.

The Hell's Angel and I got married immediately,
Me Dad and six brothers arranged it expediently.
Now he's on the run and I'm on the Deserted Wife's Pension,
I wish I'd paid Normie a bit more attention
Instead of saying:

"Rack off, Normie, you and your mates,
I know what you're after, but I'll put you straight.
I'll smash your back window with a great lump of rock."

I wish I hadn'ave told him to p-p-p-push off,
I wish I hadn'ave told him to r-r-r-rack off Normie, you and your mates.

That old Hell's Angel didn't have what it takes,
If I'd only listened when you said gidday,
We'd be happy in the back of your hot FJ,
Happy in the back of your hot FJ.
(Oh! Normie, you could'ave had me if you'd played your cards right.)

Bob Hudson and Chris Neal

Wangaratta Wahine

*Mick Conway — vocals, washboard, phonograph horn, ukulele, jug — and Dave Flett —
bass, slide dobro, vocal harmonies, ukulele — are just two of the members of the
magnificent Captain Matchbox Whoopee Band who recorded this as the title track of
their long-selling, long-playing "flat record" in 1974. Should you wish to emulate their
sound in the privacy of your own home you will also require, in addition to the
instruments listed above, a harmonica, kazoo, whistles, violin, drums, keyboards, banjo,
mandolin, guitar and an ability to tap dance.*

I walked in the roadhouse restaurant,
It had been a long time,
My mind was far away,
The lady at the counter asked me
"What do you want?"
But as I looked towards the plastic palm trees
Here's all I could say:

My Wahine in white Wangaratta
It is not goodbye, we will hula again.
My Wahine in white, it doesn't matter
That we're apart, I still love you.

Although I must go far down the road,
The Hume Highway, and trucks will pass
And gum leaves fall, I'll return some day.
She looked at me, said I was a great galoot,
Hauled her husband in who showed me the door,
Then I departed with a healthy boot, ugh,
And as I flew out the summer breeze
Seemed to whisper to me:

My Wahine in white Wangaratta
It is not goodbye, we will hula again.

Though we're apart, I still recall
The parted palm trees, the waves in her hair.
I remember the lagoon, the sink where the water falls
But most of all, I remember her husband Craig
(About six foot six, broad shoulders, what a wacker).

My Wahine in white Wangaratta
It is not goodbye, we will hula again.
My Wahine in white, it doesn't matter
That we're apart, I still love you.

Mike Conway and David Flett

THE HERO OF THE DAY

Hustling Hinkler

Born at Bundaberg in 1892, Bert Hinkler shattered many an international aviation record in his short career. His most notable flight was in 1928 when he flew from London to Darwin in just 15½ days. This was not only the fastest flight over the distance but also the longest flight ever made solo. Australia accorded him a hero's welcome and, of course, commemorated the event in song.

From coast to coast we all can boast
And sing a toast to one
Who's made a name, for being game —
He was born with wings as fine
As any bird that flies,
A lucky star guides him afar.

Chorus:
"Hustling Hinkler" up in the sky,
Fair or windy, he's flying high —
Peerless, fearless, knows ev'ry cloud,
The kind of son makes a mother feel proud.
Bustling Hinkler rides all alone
In a little plane all his own,
Hustling Hinkler showed them the way,
And he's the hero of the day.

This Aussie son set out for fun,
He had no thought of fear,
And now he's home, from o'er the foam,
The whole world's mighty proud of him,
As proud as it can be,
And now he's here let's give a cheer.

L. Wolfe Gilbert

Our Don Bradman

"Now I ask you is he any good?" At home there was no doubt on the subject when the Australian eleven left for Britain to battle for the Ashes in the 1930 Test series. Jack O'Hagan's song was written in time for the broadcasting of that series and, as Bradman stood at the wicket in the third Test at Leeds and notched up his record innings score of 334, O'Hagan himself could be heard on Melbourne radio singing his praises. He was to be joined by over 40,000 of his countrymen, most of whom purchased copies of the song within the next few days.

Who is it that all Australia raves about?
Who has won our very highest praise?
Now is it Amy Johnson, or little Mickey Mouse?
No! it's just a country lad who's bringing down the house.
And he's

Refrain:
Our Don Bradman — And I ask you is he any good?
Our Don Bradman — As a batsman he can sure lay on the wood.
For when he goes in to bat
He knocks ev'ry record flat,
For there isn't any thing he cannot do,
Our Don Bradman — Ev'ry Aussie "dips his lid" to you.

Our Don Bradman — Now I ask you is he any good?
Our Don Bradman — As a batsman he is certainly "plum pud".
Tate and Larwood meet their fate,
For it's always "shut the gate"
When the boy from Bowral hits four after four.
Our Don Bradman — Always manages to top the score.

Woodfull, Grimmett, Ponsford, Kippax and the rest,
Proved that they were equal to the best,
How gallantly and nobly, we know they've done their share,
But there's one who tops them all, a real Devil-may-care.
And he's

Our Don Bradman — And I ask you is he any good?
Our Don Bradman — As a batsman he can sure lay on the wood.
How that Mister Lyon, poor fish,
Must just sit and wish and wish,
That our Don had never come across the foam,
Our Don Bradman — What a welcome waits for you back home.

Our Don Bradman — Now I ask you is he any good?
Our Don Bradman — As a batsman he is certainly "plum pud".
Tho' those cricketers now gone.
Trumper, Spofforth and so on,
Wrote their names for ever in the Hall of Fame,
Our Don Bradman — Is the greatest ever played the game.

Jack O'Hagan

Goodbye, Phar Lap, Goodbye!

Though not strictly an All-Time Favourite, this is irresistible and you can sing it if you know the tune of "The Wearing of the Green". This tribute was sold in the streets of Melbourne after Phar Lap's death in America in April 1932.

You all know a mighty racehorse,
And how he won his fame;
He was the wonder of the turf,
And Phar Lap was his name.

With that well-known jockey,
Jim Pike upon his back,
You'd say goodnight, it's quite all right
When Phar Lap's on the track.

No doubt he was a wonder —
The best we've ever seen,
In any land or any clime,
In on or off the green.

And when he crossed the ocean
He made Australia's name;
With Billy Elliott on his back,
They surely played the game.

There's no doubt that all we Aussies
Are proud of this great horse.
There never was a better steed
That ever took the course.

Tom Woodcock should be mentioned,
The one who trained this mount
To win so many thousands,
It was getting hard to count.

But what about the owners —
The way they nursed their pet?
He was the Daddy of them all,
They've never beat him yet!

I was talking to a friend of mine
I met the other day,
He said to me, "Well, did you see
Where Phar Lap's passed away?"

"Well, I really can't believe it,"
I then unto him said.
"It must be quite a joke, that's all,
Why, Phar Lap isn't dead!"

When Australia heard the news
She sadly shook her head;
We really can't believe it yet
That Phar Lap's lying dead.

Now that we have lost him,
Our champion's gone to rest,
We bless the day he went away,
His owners thought it best.

We got the news in Melbourne,
And all felt pretty sad
To hear of Phar Lap's sudden death,
It really was too bad.

But, along with dear old Carbine,
His history cannot die,
As if he'd lived to tell the tale
They'd know the reason why!

Well, I trust that all who loved him
Just wish the same as I —
God bless our hero of the turf,
Goodbye, Phar Lap, Goodbye!

Anon.

The "Goondiwindi Grey"

*During the latter stages of his career Gunsynd, that great Australian racehorse, after walking out onto the track, would invariably stop short while the crowd applauded him. No amount of urging by the jockey would move him until he was ready.
Set to Brian Wallace's stirring music, this song commemorates Gunsynd's courageous career and his retirement in 1973. Were he alive and with you when you sang it, doubtless the gallant grey would be unmoving until the applause was over.*

Chorus:
We've cheered him from the grand-stand and
We've cheered him from the flat,
We've cheered a little beauty,
A real aris-to-crat;
He's never thrown the towel in,
Been a trier all the way,
A horse we're really proud of —
The "Goondiwindi Grey".

From Eagle Farm to Randwick and
From there to Flemington,
He chased the Tulloch record,
Winning hearts with ev'ry run;
He made it in October
On the Moonee Valley track,
Went past the post to glory,
With Higgins on his back.

A Tuesday in November
Didn't alter how we feel!
We might have torn up tickets
But we got an honest deal.
If there were cups for courage
You could trot him up for one,
For if it could be measured
I'd say he had a ton.

We'll miss him, that's for certain,
Now his saddle's put aside,
But 'round our track of mem'ries
"Gunsynd" will always stride.
A-swinging 'round the corner
And then laying back his ears —
The champ from Goondiwindi
With the champs of other years.

Nev. Hauritz

Up There Cazaly

Yes Virginia, there was a Roy Cazaly who lived 1893–1963 and played Australian
Rules football and left memories of superb moments of play to the nation. He left as well
the fascinating sound of his name. In his book Australian Heroes, Geoffrey Dutton
records: "Although by no means all Australian states play Australian Rules football, the
cry 'Up there Cazaly!' as he went up for a high mark has passed into the Australian
language. In World War II it was a greeting, an encouragement and a shout of triumph.
It is now a pop song." And the song too has passed into the Australian repertoire.
Originally written as a one-minute jingle and later expanded, the full version was sung
by its author, Mike Brady, at the 1979 VFL Grand Final. By the end of that year over
300,000 copies of the record had been sold, making "Up There Cazaly" Australia's
best-selling single in recording history.

Well you work to earn a living,
But on weekends comes the time
You can do whatever turns you on,
Get out and clear your mind.
Me I like football — there's a lot of things around,
Line 'em up together — footy wins hands down.

Up there Cazaly, in there and fight,
Out there and at 'em, show 'em your might.
Up there Cazaly, don't let 'em in,
Fly like an angel, you're out there to win.

Now there's a lot more things to football,
Than really meets the eye,
There are days when you could fly.
You either love or hate it,
Depending on the score.
When the team run out or they kick a goal,
How's the mighty roar . . .

Up there Cazaly, in there and fight,
Out there and at 'em, show 'em your might.
Up there Cazaly, don't let 'em in,
Fly like an angel, you're out there to win.

Up there Cazaly, you're out there to win,
In there and at 'em, don't let 'em in.
Up there Cazaly, show 'em your hide,
Fight like the devil,
The crowd's on your side.

Up there Cazaly, in there and fight,
Out there and at 'em, show 'em your might.
Up there Cazaly, show 'em your hide,
Fight like the devil,
The crowd's on your side . . .
The crowd's on your side . . .

Mike Brady

Come On, Aussie, Come On

While not single-handedly responsible for a decline in the popularity of Test cricket in Australia, the gently persuasive duo who head the advertising agency Mojo must be seen to have had some influence in peddling its rival attraction, the one-day matches of World Series Cricket. "Come On, Aussie, Come On", written to promote the Series, is enough to stir the most sluggish chauvinist to keep a welcome on the hillside.

Chorus:
Come on, Aussie, come on, come on.
Come on, Aussie, come on, come on.
Come on, Aussie, come on, come on.
Come on, Aussie, come on.

Lillee's pounding down like a machine.
Pascoe's making divots in the green.
Marsh is taking wickets.
Hookes is clearing pickets.
And the Chappells' eyes have got that killer gleam.

Walker's playing havoc with the bats.
Redpath, it's good to see you back.
Laird is making runs.
Doug is chewing gum.
And Gilmour's wielding willow like an axe.

Coda:
Mister,
You've been training all the winter, and there's not a team that's fitter.
And that's the way it's got to be.
'Cause you're up against the best, you know.
This is a super test, you know.
And you've got to beat the best the world has seen.

Allan Johnston and Alan Morris

Here Come the Aussies

In 1972, Ian Chappell's eleven went to "bring the Ashes home again". Well, they tried, but the two teams tied and thus the sacred relic of the MCC stumps was shared that year. However, while in England the team recorded this war chant. It was a rollicking, thumping great success and, amid the rollick and thump, nobody seemed to mind the failure of the lads' predictions.

Here on the pitch, whether rain or fine,
We can shine all the time.
Home or away, come and see us play,
You're welcome every day.

Chorus:
Here come the Aussies
And cricket is the game,
We're all together and
Winning is our aim,
So we'll play on through the English rain,
And win the Ashes back again.

Daniel Boone and Rod McQueen

83

CAME THE WORD
ONE FATEFUL DAY

Little Boy Lost

*On 5 February 1960 whilst out in the backblocks of his home farm in the rugged
New England ranges, four-year-old Stephen Walls wandered off and disappeared. One
of the largest land and air searches ever mounted in Australia found the boy three-and-a-
half days later. Incredibly, in such hostile terrain, Stephen was still alive.
Johnny Ashcroft adds a personal note on the song: "It so happened that in my wild and
wicked youth, I was a professional trapper working out of Kangaroo Camp, near Guyra
so I understood the type of country in which the search took place. Also at the time that
Stephen was lost, I had a boy who was almost the same age so the feelings of the parents
were that much easier to understand. The song is written as a tribute to the 5000 people
who cared enough about the welfare of one small boy to mount such a massive search."*

In the wild New England ranges came the word one fateful day,
To every town and village, that a boy had lost his way.
All the town's folk quickly gathered and the wild bush horses tossed,
As they went to search the ranges for a little boy lost,
They went to search the ranges for a little boy lost.

A lad of just four summers, Stephen Walls, that is his name,
And nobody doubts his courage, 'cause he's hardy and he's game,
But there's danger in this country that man has seldom crossed,
And they wonder if they'll find alive this little boy lost,
And they wonder if they'll find alive this little boy lost.

Came the night, came the morning. Another night, another dawning,
And a mother weeps in silence as she kneels before the Cross,
And she prays to God in heaven for her little boy lost,
And she prays to God in heaven for her little boy lost.

The little town's deserted, no-one walks upon the street,
For they comb the wild bush country on a thousand aching feet.
They searched ev'ry hidden valley though his trail they never crossed,
And their hopes are slowly fading for this little boy lost,
And their hopes are slowly fading for this little boy lost.

The blazing sun beat down upon the earth that final day,
With heavy hearts they prayed to God above to show the way.
When from a scrubby gully came the voice they've ne'er forgot,
"Where's my daddy, where's my daddy?" cried the little boy lost,
"Where's my daddy, where's my daddy?" cried the little boy lost.

In the far New England ranges there's a boy that's known so well,
There's a story that the town's folk and the bushmen often tell:
How he fought a rugged country, where man has seldom crossed;
And a mother's prayers were answered for her little boy lost.

Johnny Ashcroft

Santa Never Made It into Darwin

Early on Christmas Day 1974 a cyclone of devastating force hit Darwin. After five hours of winds exceeding 200 kilometres per hour, many lives were lost and about 90 per cent of the city buildings were destroyed. An Australia-wide Darwin relief appeal was immediately launched. This song was a response both to the tragedy and to the appeal, as Bill Cate recalls: "The inspiration to write the song came from a question from my then eight-year-old daughter Samantha. When she heard the news reports she asked me 'What happened to the kids' Christmas in Darwin?' and I replied 'Santa never made it into Darwin'. I continued with this idea and within the hour had written the song." Bill and Boyd appeared the next day on a telethon appeal and performed the song. The response was tremendous, with calls coming in from all over Australia. Royalties from the subsequent recording were donated to the Darwin appeal — a not insubstantial contribution as the record topped the charts almost immediately and remained there for many weeks.

On Christmas eve of '74 the warning sounded out.
On all the broadcast stations a great storm was near about.
The boys and girls asleep in bed, tomorrow was their day,
Their mums and dads all prayed the mighty storm would turn away.

Santa never made it into Darwin,
Disaster struck at dawn on Christmas day.
Santa never made it into Darwin,
A big wind came and blew the town away.

Christmas morning was a nightmare as cyclone Tracy struck,
It ripped apart the buildings like an atom bomb had struck.
It twisted iron girders, and it flattened all the trees,
The might of such a cyclone must be seen to be believed.

Many boats put out to sea, very few returned,
Most were pounded on the rocks or in huge seas overturned.
Australia was shocked and saddened as the news came through,
A devastated city that must be built anew,
For suffering and heartbreak to happen in this way,
A natural disaster to come on Christmas day.

Bill Cate

ORANA TO CHRISTMAS DAY

Learnt by generations of school children, the carols of John Wheeler and William James give Australians their own perspective of Christmas time. Here is a reverence as much for the Australian bush and outback as for the Christmas story.

Composer William James was the first Federal Director of the Australian Broadcasting Commission and collaborated with John Wheeler on three sets of carols, each of five songs, which were published between 1948 and 1961. Those presented here are from the earliest set.

The notes accompanying each carol are from the Programme Notes written by the authors for one of their many performances. They also wrote: "It is not suggested that these new carols should take the place of those we have all known from childhood: but the carols of other countries owe much to the local background of the places that produced them, and Australians feel it is fitting that they should have their own carols, with their own local colour; because though it is midwinter the other side of the Equator at Christmas time, in Australia it is midsummer."

Christmas bush, clear summer skies, triumphant birdsong — truly something to sing about.

Christmas Day

"This carol gives vivid expression to typical Christmas Day weather in Australia, when the burning north wind blows the red dust from the arid inlands. The music captures the spirit of joy which is the true message of Christmas."

The north-wind is tossing the leaves,
The red dust is over the town;
The sparrows are under the eaves,
And the grass in the paddock is brown;
As we lift up our voices and sing
To the Christ-Child the Heavenly King.

The tree-ferns in green gullies sway;
The cool stream flows silently by:
The joy-bells are greeting the day,
And the chimes are a-drift in the sky,
As we lift up our voices and sing
To the Christ-Child, the Heavenly King.

John Wheeler

The Three Drovers

"An original little fantasy of Christmas night on the great Australian plains, far away from town and city, in which three cattle drovers see the Star of the East, and hear the angelic choir. In his setting the composer vividly suggests the horsemen riding on their starlit way.

Note: One of the most familiar spectacles of the Australian night sky, is the luminous galaxy of stars known as the 'Milky Way'."

Across the plains one Christmas night,
Three drovers riding blythe and gay,
Looked up and saw a starry light,
More radiant than the Milky Way;
And on their hearts such wonder fell,
They sang with joy "Noel! Noel!
Noel! Noel! Noel!"

The air was dry with summer heat,
And smoke was on the yellow moon;
But from the heavens, faint and sweet,
Came floating down a wond'rous tune;
And, as they heard, they sang full well,
Those drovers three — "Noel! Noel!
Noel! Noel! Noel!"

The black swans flew across the sky,
The wild dog called across the plain,
The starry lustre blazed on high,
Still echoed on the heavenly strain;
And still they sang "Noel! Noel!"
Those drovers three — "Noel! Noel!
Noel! Noel! Noel!"

John Wheeler

The Silver Stars Are in the Sky

"A mother sings a slumber-song by the light of the Christmas moon. This little carol with its haunting melody has already become a great favourite.

Note: The Boo-Book is a small Australian owl whose rhythmic call is heard throughout the night. Paddock — a familiar word applied to what, in other countries, is a field enclosed by a fence."

The silver stars are in the sky,
The red-gold moon is riding high,
O, sleep, my little one, sleep!

Once long ago against her breast,
A mother hush'd a babe to rest
Who was the Prince of Heav'n above,
The Lord of gentleness and love,
O, sleep, my little one, sleep.

The boo-book calls across the night,
The brown moths flutter in the light,
O, sleep, my little one, sleep!

In Bethlehem long, long ago,
When roads and paddocks gleam'd with snow;
On this same night, that mother mild
Lull'd into dreams her royal Child.
So, sleep, my little one, sleep!

John Wheeler

Carol of the Birds

"Another little Christmas fantasy, where words and music combine to give us a happy picture of carolling birds.

Note: The Brolga is the Australian Crane, one of Australia's largest birds. It is usually found in pairs or flocks out on the plains or in swamp areas. Brolgas amuse themselves by dancing, forming 'quadrille parties'. All manner of movements are performed in a most graceful way. Bell-birds — the tuneful tinkling notes of this small bird have inspired many Australian poets. Friar-birds — there are several different species of this bird, most of which are found in the north of the continent. They feed on berries, native fruits and 'nectar of flowers'. Currawongs or Bell-Magpies — one of this species calls 'curre-wong, curre-wong' while on the wing. Lorikeets — just one of the large family of Australian parrots."

Out on the plains the Brolgas are dancing,
Lifting their feet like war-horses prancing,
Up to the sun the Wood-larks go winging,
Faint in the dawn light echoes their singing —
"ORANA! ORANA! Orana to Christmas Day."

Down where the tree-ferns grow by the river,
There where the waters sparkle and quiver,
Deep in the gullies Bell-birds are chiming,
Softly and sweetly their lyric notes rhyming —
"ORANA! ORANA! Orana to Christmas Day."

Friar-birds sip the nectar of flowers,
Currawongs chant in wattle-tree bowers,
In the blue ranges Lorikeets calling —
Carols of bushbirds rising and falling —
"ORANA! ORANA! Orana to Christmas Day."

John Wheeler

Christmas Bush for His Adorning

"The inspiration for this carol is a distinctive feature of the Australian Christmas, for then every home is decorated with its slim, graceful leaves and tiny red flowers. Once again words and music joyously blend in a note of triumph for the birth of the Saviour of the World."

All the bells are gaily ringing,
Birds in every tree are singing;
Let us in the golden weather,
Gather Christmas Bush together.

Christ is born! The angels thunder
Thro' the Heav'ns their tale of wonder,
While we pluck, for His adorning,
Christmas Bush this hallow'd morning.

Christ has conquer'd Evil's pow'r,
Hear the bells rock ev'ry tow'r;
Birds and beasts lift up their voices,
Freed at last the world rejoices.

Onward with triumphant chorus,
Following the road before us,
Singing thro' the golden weather,
Gath'ring Christmas Bush together.

John Wheeler

Six White Boomers

Rolf writes: "I had always been amazed that in my home town of Perth in Christmas temperatures of 90 to 100° Fahrenheit, we were singing songs about Jingle Bells and snow and ice." As a result he got together with friend John D. Brown to write this song — "an Australian Christmas song based on an old Australian Christmas legend which we'd written the previous week."

Perhaps the stuff of truer legend is found in Rolf's discovery of the amazing instrument on which he accompanies his singing of this and many other songs. Rolf remembers a portrait he was to paint and recalls preparing a piece of hardboard with a background colour, placing it on a heater to dry then, before his subject arrived, having to fan it to cool it. "...And there was this marvellous sound...it seemed to have its own rhythm." The portrait was finished but never given to its subject. Rolf used it as background to a recording released in mid 1960 which was an immediate success. Thus was the wobbleboard introduced to the world.

Early on one Christmas Day, a Joey
   kangaroo
Was far from home and lost in a great big
   zoo.
"Mummy, where's my mummy,
   they've taken her away."
"We'll help you find your mummy, son,
   hop up on the sleigh."

Up beside the bag of toys, little Joey hopped,
But they hadn't gone far when Santa stopped,
Unharnessed all the reindeer,
   and Joey wondered why,
Then he heard a far off booming in the sky.

Chorus:
Six white boomers, snow white boomers
Racing Santa Claus through the blazing sun,
Six white boomers, snow white boomers,
On his Australian run.

Pretty soon old Santa began to feel the heat,
Took his fur-lined boots off to cool his feet,
Into one popped Joey, feeling quite O.K.,
While those old man kangaroos kept pulling
   on the sleigh.

Joey said to Santa, "Santa what
   about the toys?
Aren't you giving some to these girls and
   boys?"
"They've all got their presents son, we were
   here last night,
This trip is an extra trip, Joey's special
   flight."

Soon the sleigh was flashing past, right over
   Marble Bar,
"Slow down there," cried Santa. "It can't be
   far,
Come up on my lap here son, and have a
   look around,"
"There she is, that's Mummy, bounding up
   and down."

Well that's the bestest Christmas treat that
   Joey ever had,
Curled up in mother's pouch all snug and
   glad,
The last they saw was Santa heading
   northward from the sun,
The only year the boomers worked a double
   run.

Rolf Harris and John D. Brown

COME,
OLD MOTHER
HUBBARD

My Pal Skippy

It took an expatriate Englishman to write one of the best-known children's songs of the TV era. Eric Jupp points out that the Skippy song used for the television show is in fact only two lines repeated. His longer song about Skippy is charming but it is less well-known and so the music has been included.

FROM THE TELEVISION SERIES
"SKIPPY, THE BUSH KANGAROO."

98

Kangaroo Song

Annie R. Rentoul wrote many stories and poems for young Australians, possibly the best of which were included in two magnificent books Elves and Fairies *and* Fairyland *illustrated by her sister Ida Rentoul Outhwaite.*
Set to Georgette Peterson's music, the "Kangaroo Song" has become a perennial favourite. Generations of Australians, brought up on the ABC Kindergarten of the Air, will be able to sing along — perhaps even hop along.
Are you ready? Paws up! Now, one, two, three...

Old Bumpety Jumpety Hop-and-Go-One
Was lying at ease on his side in the sun,
And this old kangaroo, he was whisking the flies
With his glossy long tail, from his coat and his eyes.

Chorus:
Bumpety Jumpety Hop-and-Go-One,
Hop-and-Go-One, Hop-and-Go-One,
Sleep with an eye open out in the sun,
Bumpety Jumpety Hop.

He was wild in his youth was this old kangaroo,
And learnt from experience all that he knew.
He could tackle a rabbiter's pack, one and all,
For they often had hunted him, when he was small.

Now foolish young Frisky, the woodcutter's dog,
Came peeping at Bumpety over a log,
So it's "Up boys and at 'im!" he barked to the pack.
And "Right! we are coming!" the others barked back.

I wish you had seen how old Bumpety stood
And boxed all their ears in the heart of the wood!
And he hopped off in triumph as soon as he'd done,
So we'll all cry "Hurroosha!" for Hop-and-Go-One.

Annie R. Rentoul

ABC Children's Session Opening Song

To almost everyone who grew up in Australia in the 1940s and '50s there are three songs that stir strong memories of childhood. We see ourselves sitting entranced before the bakelite box housing the wireless set — perhaps later replaced by a radiogram — listening to the ABC Children's Session with its opening and closing songs and, of course, the Argonauts' song. Remember the pledge, the Band of Happy Rowers, the Dragon's Tooth Certificate and the elusive Golden Fleece?
In her book Happy Rowing *Ida Elizabeth Jenkins, "Elizabeth", records the ease with which she dashed off these gems one night in 1939 (for the opening and closing songs) and another night in 1941 for the Argonauts' song. She adds: "From time to time I hear the old Children's Session theme recordings played by one or other of the lively lads of ABC radio and I rub my hands, knowing that another few cents will be set aside for me at the Australian Performing Rights Association." Well rowed "Elizabeth", and our thanks.*

Come, Old Mother Hubbard, and Jack and Jill,
And Tom the Piper's son,
Leave your troubles, forget your spill,
We're going to have some fun!

The wireless says to hurry and run
To leave your games and toys;
The wireless says the time has come
For all the girls and boys.

So come with a hop, a skip and a run,
It's time for the Session, it's time for the fun.

Ida Elizabeth Jenkins

The Argonauts' Club Song

Fifty mighty Argonauts, bending to the oars,
Today will go adventuring to yet uncharted shores.
Fifty young adventurers today set forth and so
We cry with Jason "Man the boats, and Row! Row! Row!"

Row! Row! Merry oarsmen, Row!
That dangers lie ahead we know, we know.
But bend with all your might
As you sail into the night
And wrong will bow to right.
"Jason" cry, adventure know,
Argonauts Row! Row! Row!

Ida Elizabeth Jenkins

Kookaburra Sits in the Old Gum Tree

Sung in the form of a round, this cheerful ditty has been on infants'-school curriculae since education first established itself in the colony.

Kookaburra sits in the old gum tree,
Merry, merry king of the bush is he.
Laugh kookaburra, laugh kookaburra,
Gay your life must be.

Anon.

ABC Children's Session Goodnight Song

A jolly goodnight to you and you,
And you and you and you,
The time has come to finish
And our Session now is through.
The thought is as old as old as old
But the wish tonight is new,
A jolly goodnight to everyone,
A jolly goodnight to everyone,
A jolly goodnight to all,
Especially you, and you, and you...and you!

Ida Elizabeth Jenkins

KEEP PLAYING 'TIL I SHOOT THRO', BLUE

Tie Me Kangaroo Down, Sport

Many good things Australian have originated in Britain — the majority of Australians for example. It should therefore come as little surprise that this, the most dinkum of Australian ditties, was written in the Sceptred Isle. It was the mid 1950s and Rolf Harris was entertaining fellow expatriates at London's Down Under Club. He recalls hearing a piece of Belafonte calypso, which inspired the title, and thereafter being consumed with the fever of composition which was fashioned "in the traditional way — on the back of a menu".

"Sounds like a load of old nonsense to me," his father-in-law was heard to say when Rolf tried out the song in private, and its first public audience "booed it off the stage". But it was this song that eventually took Rolf (and his family) around the world many, many times and into the ken of "nonsense" lovers everywhere.

Recitation:
There's an old Australian stockman,
Lying dying, and he gets himself up on
  one elbow,
And he turns to his mates who are
  gathered 'round him
And he says:—

Watch me wallaby's feed, mate,
Watch me wallaby's feed.
They're a dangerous breed, mate,
So watch me wallaby's feed.
Altogether now!

Chorus:
Tie me kangaroo down, sport,
Tie me kangaroo down.
Tie me kangaroo down, sport,
Tie me kangaroo down.

Keep me cockatoo cool, Curl,
Keep me cockatoo cool.
Don't go acting the fool, Curl,
Just keep me cockatoo cool.
Altogether now!

Take me koala back, Jack,
Take me koala back.
He lives somewhere out on the track, Mac,
So take me koala back.
Altogether now!

Let me abos go loose, Lew,
Let me abos go loose.
They're of no further use, Lew,
So let me abos go loose.
Altogether now!

Mind me platypus duck, Bill,
Mind me platypus duck.
Don't let him go running amok, Bill,
Mind me platypus duck.
Altogether now!

Play your didgeridoo, Blue,
Play your didgeridoo.
Keep playing 'til I shoot thro', Blue,
Play your didgeridoo.
Altogether now!

Tan me hide when I'm dead, Fred,
Tan me hide when I'm dead.
So we tanned his hide when he died, Clyde,
(Spoken)
And that's it hanging on the shed.
Altogether now!

Rolf Harris

We Love Football, Meat Pies, Kangaroos and Holden Cars

The title says it all.

All:
We love football, meat pies, kangaroos and Holden cars.
Football, meat pies, kangaroos and Holden cars.

Announcer:
That's football, meat pies, kangaroos and Holden cars.

All:
Football and meat pies, kangaroos and Holden cars.

Announcer:
I think you'd better tell me again.

All:
We love football, meat pies, kangaroos and Holden cars.

Announcer:
In case you're wondering,
This commercial is brought to you by
Football, meat pies, kangaroos and Australia's own car.

All:
They go together
Underneath the southern star,
Football and meat pies, kangaroos and Holden cars.

Announcer:
Makes sense to me.

All:
Football, meat pies, kangaroos and Holden cars.

That's the Way to Spell Woolloomooloo

Isadore Brodsky in his Sydney's Little World of Woolloomooloo *recalls a time when spelling bees were still a favoured parlour pastime early in the century and the following two song versions offered guidance in the spelling of Woolloomooloo. Brodsky writes: "Because there is only one L difference the less fastidious will not care which spelling is finally adopted. Perfectionists will continue to think otherwise."*

W double O, L double O, M double O, LO, O,
Upon my word 'tis true
That's the way to spell Wooloomooloo.
Now I bet a dollar
There isn't a scholar
Can spell that right first go:
W double O, L double O, M double O, LO, O.

"...for that's the way, you see,
The way to spell Woolloomooloo.
Now I'll bet a dollar
There isn't a scholar
To spell it right first go:
W double O, double L, double O,
M double O, LO, O."

Anon.

Red-back on the Toilet Seat

"I hope there's no red-backs down here, because the bloody light's not working again!"
Mike Kodra to Slim Newton, Perth, 1969.
Some of the most memorable hit songs are those that arrive "out of the blue" and are in
striking contrast to the run of musical trends of their time. In 1972, Slim Newton's
recording of the Redback on the Toilet Seat *became one of those songs, and because*
most Australians could remember the traditional outhouse and its potential dangers, it
also became part of our Australian culture.

There was a red-back on the toilet seat
When I was there last night,
I didn't see him in the dark,
But boy! I felt his bite!
I jumped high up into the air,
And when I hit the ground,
That crafty red-back spider
Wasn't nowhere to be found.

Chorus:
There was a red-back on the toilet seat
When I was there last night,
I didn't see him in the dark,
But boy! I felt his bite!
And now I'm here in hospital,
A sad and sorry plight,
And I curse the red-back spider
On the toilet seat last night.

Rushed in to the missus,
Told her just where I'd been bit,
She grabbed the cut-throat razor blade,
And I nearly took a fit.
I said "Just forget what's on your mind,
And call a doctor please,
'Cause I've got a feeling that your cure
Is worse than the disease."

I can't lay down, I can't sit up,
And I don't know what to do,
And all the nurses think it's funny,
But that's not my point of view.
I tell you it's embarrassing,
(And that's to say the least)
That I'm too sick to eat a bite,
While that spider had a feast!

And when I get back home again,
I tell you what I'll do,
I'll make that red-back suffer
For the pain I'm going through.
I've had so many needles
That I'm looking like a sieve,
And I promise you that spider
Hasn't very long to live!

Slim Newton

The Snake Gully Swagger

Jack O'Hagan dominated the Australian songwriting scene for the first half of this century. "The Snake Gully Swagger" is just one of over 200 published songs he has to his credit and, like this one, most were hits of their time. Some, however, have endured longer. In this collection there are six O'Hagan songs — "Where the Dog Sits on the Tucker Box", "Along the Road to Gundagai", "Hustling Hinkler", "God Bless Australia", "Our Don Bradman" and "The Snake Gully Swagger". Jack O'Hagan dominates Australian songwriting still.

What's all this talk about the Lambeth Walk?
Why, we've got a dance got it beat a mile.
It's bonzer, it's classy 'n full of style,
It's all the rage with folks of ev'ry age,
It's easy to do and it's as catchy as the flu.

Everybody round the place will dance to it,
It's goin' to set the pace so prance to it,
It's a snifter body lifter the Snake Gully Swagger.
Every tramp along the road can sway to it,
And farmers help to load the dray to it,
Even abos and their tabbos
Do the Snake Gully Swagger,
Even old maids so prim are gettin' into trim
By doing it now,
And Ted Ramsay's out, despite a touch of gout,
Doin' steps with his wife I vow.
Everybody in the land will sing to it
And ev'ry rhythm band will swing to it,
There's a possie — in our Aussie
For the Snake Gully Swagger.

Ev'ry little woolly lamb goes baaa'a to it,
And laughing jacks go ooha-ha to it,
It's a winner on the chinner the Snake Gully Swagger.
Pretty birdies in the trees tweet-tweet to it,
And even billy goats can bleat to it,
It's a dandy — knocks 'em bandy —
The Snake Gully Swagger.
All the pigs in the pens, the roosters and the hens,
Are doing it now.
The ducks and drakes are doin' shimmy shakes,
Even Sally our champeen cow.
Grab your partner round the waist and go to it,
With ev'ry step she takes she'll glow to it —
It's a spry dance, dinky-di dance,
The Snake Gully Swagger.

Jack O'Hagan

Stompin' at Maroubra

*Joe Halford and Jay Justin had some inkling that their 1963 toe-tapper would be
popular. Joe writes: "Prior to my production of the record for EMI, Jay and I joined
Little Pattie and The Statesmen at Maroubra for rehearsals. During the initial run
through of the song a crowd began to gather around, and before long they were stompin'
to the music every time the song was played. The same thing happened with the other
side of the record "He's My Blond-Headed, Stompie Wompie, Real Gone Surfer Boy".
Happily the initial impact followed through to the public at large." Happily indeed —
Joe, Jay and Little Pattie found themselves the proud parents of a double-sided
chart-stopping hit.*

There's a dance that they're doin' down Maroubra way,
The surfies and the sandies will make it stay.
Feel that rhythm, you can feel that beat,
All you gotta do is move your feet, and go...

Chorus:
Stomp, stomp, stompin' at Maroubra.
Stomp, stomp, stompin' at Maroubra.
Stomp, stomp, stompin' at Maroubra.
Everybody's doin' the Maroubra stomp.

Well all you gotta have is your stompin' shoes.
You can really stomp right away your blues.
Up and down and all around, yeah they're really coming
From all over the town to go...

So come on let's head down Maroubra way.
You can keep a-stompin' till the break of day.
Grab your baby, take him by the hand,
Join the party down on the sand and go...

Joe Halford and Jay Justin

Shaddap You Face

Bravo, bravissimo Joe! The Anglo-Saxons and that excessively musical tribe the Celts can't have it all their own way — the Mediterranean makes an appearance at last. Joe's cheeky hit of 1980 may have perplexed serious musicologists, but gave pleasure to many. So, Vivaldi, Verdi, Puccini, Rossini — shaddap you faces, eh?

(*Spoken*)
'Allo, I'm-a Giuseppe, I got-a something special-a for you. Ready? Uno,
    duo, tre, quatro!

When I was a boy,
Just about the eighth-a grade,
Mama used to say:
"Don't stay out late with the bad-a boys,
Always shoot-a pool
(*Spoken*)
Giuseppe going to flunk-a school!"

Chorus:
What's-a matter you? Hey!
Got-a no respect,
What-a you t'ink you do?
Why you look-a so sad?
It's-a not so bad,
It's-a a nice-a place, ah,
Shad-dap-a you face!
(*Spoken*)
That's-a my mama, I can remember!
Big accordion solo! Ah!
Play dat again!
Really nice, really nice!
Mama, she said it all-a da time!

Boy, it make-a me sick,
All the t'ing I gotta do,
I can't get-a no kicks,
Always got to follow rules,
Boy, it make-a me sick,
Just to make-a lousy bucks,
(*Spoken*)
Got to feel-a like a fool,
And-a mama used to say all-a time:

Soon-a come a day,
Gonna be a big-a star,
(*Spoken*)
Den I make-a TV shows and-a movies,
Get-a myself a new car,
But still I be myself,
I don't want-a to change a t'ing,
Still a-dance and a-sing,
I t'ink about-a mama, she used to say:

Monologue:
Hello, everybody
'At's out-a dere in-a radio and-a TV land,
Did you know I had a big-a hit-a song in-a Italy with-a dis?
"Shaddap-a you face",
I sing-a dis-a song, all-a my fans applaud,
Dey clap-a da hands,
Dat-a make me feel-a so good;
You ought to learn-a dis-a song,
It's-a real-a simple —
See, I sing: "What's-a matter you?"
You sing: "Hey!"
Den I sing-a da rest,
And den at de end, we can all-a sing:
"Ah, Shaddap-a you face!"
OK, Let's-a try it, really big —
Uno, duo, tre, quatro!

Joe Dolce

My Boomerang Won't Come Back

Remember Charlie Drake — four foot and a couple of inches (untranslatable into a metric measure or we'll lose him)? Baby-faced and baby-voiced, this diminutive British comedian topped the pops both at home (his) and abroad (ours) with this piece of nonsense from the early 1960s.

In the bad backlands of Australia many years ago,
The Aborigine tribes were meeting having a bit pow pow.
Oom jac-ca hy-a-tum oom jac-ca hy-a-tum.

Chorus:
My boomerang won't come back,
My boomerang won't come back,
I'm a big disgrace, t' the Aborigine race,
My boomerang won't come back.

Banished him from the tribe then and sent him on his way.
He had a backless boomerang so here he could not stay.
Oom jac-ca hy-a-tum oom jac-ca hy-a-tum

Three long months he sat there, or maybe it was four.
Then an old, old man in a kangaroo skin came a knockin' at his door.
Oom jac-ca hy-a-tum oom jac-ca hy-a-tum.

Charlie Drake and Max Diamond

The Aeroplane Jelly Song

This, the longest-running singing commercial in Australia, was first aired in 1938. The song was originally sung by five-year-old Joy King who triumphed over hundreds of contestants in a competition to find a promoter of the pint-sized generation. Nearly half a century later the song still serves the Aeroplane Jelly people both on radio and television and several requests a week for the record or the music are received at Aeroplane Jelly headquarters.

I've got a song that won't take very long,
Quite a good sort of note if I strike it...
It is something we eat, and I think it's quite sweet,
And I know you are going to like it.

Chorus:
I like Aeroplane Jelly...Aeroplane Jelly for me,
I like it for dinner, I like it for tea,
A little each day is a good recipe.
The quality's high as the name will imply,
And it's made from pure fruits, one more good reason why
I like Aeroplane Jelly...Aeroplane Jelly for me.

Anon.

We're Happy Little Vegemites

In its long and glorious history as Australia's own and favourite spread, there was a time when Vegemite was called "Parwill". Here was a positive-sounding product to stand its ground beside the tentative suggestion of the opposition's Marmite. Such fun with puns is also evident many years later in the well-loved Vegemite jingle. Written by Alan Weeks, the jingle was used in the first Vegemite television commercials in 1956 and, until 1978, was a part of all radio and television advertising for the product. Spreading the word indeed — or wording the spread?

We're happy little Vegemites, as bright as bright can be,
We all enjoy our Vegemite for breakfast, lunch and tea.
Our Mummy says we're growing stronger every single week,
Because we love our Vegemite, we all adore our Vegemite —
It puts a rose in every cheek.

Alan Weeks

Farewell Aunty Jack

*In 1974 the ABC was invaded by a big, fat, jolly and extremely lethal pantomime
dame. A little maiming quickly persuaded programmers to surrender a weekly half-hour
to the lady. Thus was the nation introduced to Aunty Jack and her theme song.
OK you lot — get it right — unless you fancy a little 'armless fun.*

Farewell Aunty Jack, we know you'll be back.
Though you're ten feet tall
You don't scare us at all.
You're big, bold and tough,
But you're not so rough.
There's a scream as you plummet away.

She rides a black bike
And drives through the night.
She's big, round and fat,
But don't dare tell her that
'Cause she turns so mean
Her glove starts to gleam
And she'll scream as she plummets away.

Oh we really, really love you
And we think the world about you,
Please come back to our house
Please come back dear Aunty Jack.
Now you've gone away and left me,
Aunty Jack, please don't forget me,
Just remember I'll be waiting
At the gate dear Aunty Jack.
Yes I think I must be dreaming,
I can hear your bike a-screaming
And I know you're coming near me
Now you're back dear Aunty Jack.

Oh farewell Aunty Jack,
Do you know you'll be back?
Though you're ten feet tall
You don't scare us at all.
You're big, bold and tough,
But you're not so rough.
There's a scream as you plummet away.

Graeme Bond and Rory O'Donohue

Index of First Lines